Using the Results
of a National
Assessment of
Educational
Achievement

National Assessments of Educational Achievement

VOLUME 5

Using the Results of a National Assessment of Educational Achievement

Thomas Kellaghan
Vincent Greaney
T. Scott Murray

THE WORLD BANK
Washington, DC

© 2009 The International Bank for Reconstruction and Development / The World Bank
1818 H Street, NW
Washington, DC 20433
Telephone: 202-473-1000
Internet: www.worldbank.org
E-mail: feedback@worldbank.org

All rights reserved
1 2 3 4 12 11 10 09

This volume is a product of the staff of the International Bank for Reconstruction and Development / The World Bank. The findings, interpretations, and conclusions expressed in this volume do not necessarily reflect the views of the Executive Directors of The World Bank or the governments they represent.

The World Bank does not guarantee the accuracy of the data included in this work. The boundaries, colors, denominations, and other information shown on any map in this work do not imply any judgement on the part of The World Bank concerning the legal status of any territory or the endorsement or acceptance of such boundaries.

Rights and Permissions

The material in this publication is copyrighted. Copying and/or transmitting portions or all of this work without permission may be a violation of applicable law. The International Bank for Reconstruction and Development / The World Bank encourages dissemination of its work and will normally grant permission to reproduce portions of the work promptly.

For permission to photocopy or reprint any part of this work, please send a request with complete information to the Copyright Clearance Center Inc., 222 Rosewood Drive, Danvers, MA 01923, USA; telephone: 978-750-8400; fax: 978-750-4470; Internet: www.copyright.com.

All other queries on rights and licenses, including subsidiary rights, should be addressed to the Office of the Publisher, The World Bank, 1818 H Street, NW, Washington, DC 20433, USA; fax: 202-522-2422; e-mail: pubrights@worldbank.org.

Cover design: Naylor Design, Washington, DC

ISBN: 978-0-8213-7929-5
eISBN: 978-0-8213-7966-0
DOI: 10.1596/978-0-8213-7929-5

Library of Congress Cataloging-in-Publication Data
Kellaghan, Thomas.
　Using the results of a national assessment of educational achievement / Thomas Kellaghan, Vincent Greaney, T. Scott Murray.
　　p. cm. — (National assessments of educational achievement ; v. 5)
　Includes bibliographical references and index.
　　ISBN 978-0-8213-7929-5 (alk. paper) — ISBN 978-0-8213-7966-0 (electronic)
　1. Educational tests and measurements. 2. Achievement tests. 3. Education and state. I. Greaney, Vincent. II. Murray, T. Scott. III. Title.
　LB3051.K189 2009
　371.26′2—dc22
　　　　　　　　　　　　　　　　　　　　　　　　　　　　　　　　　2009009954

CONTENTS

FOREWORD — xi

ACKNOWLEDGMENTS — xiii

ABBREVIATIONS — xv

1. **FACTORS AFFECTING THE USE AND NONUSE OF NATIONAL ASSESSMENT FINDINGS** — 1
   - The Political Context of a National Assessment — 3
   - Accountability — 5
   - The Quality of the Assessment Instrument — 15
   - Type of Assessment — 17
   - Underuse of National Assessment Findings — 20
   - Conclusion — 24

2. **REPORTING A NATIONAL ASSESSMENT: THE MAIN REPORT** — 29
   - Context of the National Assessment — 31
   - Objectives of the National Assessment — 31
   - Framework for the National Assessment — 32
   - Procedures in Administration of the National Assessment — 32
   - Description of Achievement in the National Assessment — 33
   - Correlates of Achievement — 37
   - Change in Achievement Over Time — 42
   - Conclusion — 45

3. REPORTING A NATIONAL ASSESSMENT: OTHER INSTRUMENTS TO COMMUNICATE FINDINGS — 47
Product Specification Sheet — 48
Briefing Ministers and Senior Policy Personnel — 49
Publishing Summary Reports — 50
Publishing Technical Reports — 53
Publishing Thematic Reports — 56
Securing Media Reports — 56
Issuing Press Releases — 58
Holding Press Conferences — 62
Conducting Individual Briefings — 63
Posting Web Site Reports — 63
Making Assessment Data Available — 64
Other Dissemination Instruments — 66
Conclusion — 67

4. TRANSLATING ASSESSMENT FINDINGS INTO POLICY AND ACTION — 69
Institutional Capacity to Absorb and Use Information — 70
Trustworthiness and Relevance of Information Provided by an Assessment — 71
Procedures to Identify Appropriate Policy or Action Following an Assessment — 71
Determination of a Systemwide or Targeted Intervention — 75
Complexity of Policy Formation and Decision Making — 76
Conclusion — 77

5. NATIONAL ASSESSMENT FINDINGS, POLICY, AND EDUCATIONAL MANAGEMENT — 79
Describing Achievement — 80
Describing Resources — 81
Monitoring Achievement — 82
Reviewing the Education System — 84
Formulating General Policy and Assisting in Decision Making — 84
Setting Standards — 88
Providing Resources to Schools — 90
Supporting Curriculum Revision — 92
Revising Textbooks — 94
Conclusion — 95

CONTENTS | vii

6. **NATIONAL ASSESSMENT FINDINGS AND TEACHING**   97
   Teachers' Professional Development   98
   Focus on Schools and Classroom Teaching   108
   Conclusion   121

7. **NATIONAL ASSESSMENT FINDINGS AND PUBLIC AWARENESS**   125
   Examples of the Use of Assessment Results to Inform the Public   127
   The Role of the Media   129
   Developing a Communication Strategy   130
   Conclusion   132

8. **TOWARD OPTIMIZING THE USE AND VALUE OF NATIONAL ASSESSMENTS**   135
   Optimizing the Use of National Assessment Findings   137
   Developing National Assessments to Increase Their Value   139
   Conclusion   146

REFERENCES   147

INDEX   163

BOXES

1.1	Issues on Which a National Assessment Can Throw Light	2
1.2	Evaluating Achievement on Limited Evidence	8
1.3	The Negative Effect of High-Stakes Accountability Uses	10
1.4	Assigning Accountability for Student Achievement	13
1.5	Shifting the Blame for School Failure	13
1.6	Two Uses of Data from an International Assessment	20
1.7	Extent of Use of National Assessment Results, Honduras	21
3.1	Summary Report of Illinois State Grade 4 Students' Reading Achievement Levels on the 2007 NAEP: United States	51
3.2	Suggestions for Applying the PISA Approach to Teaching and Learning Mathematics: Ireland	52
3.3	Press Release Excerpt, NAEP: United States	60
3.4	Sample News Release: United States	61
3.5	Web Site, Mathematics Achievement in Primary Schools: Ireland	64
3.6	Site Map, NAEP Web Site: United States	65

5.1	Using Assessment Results to Promote Reforms: Dominican Republic	86
5.2	Myths about Education in the United States	87
6.1	Place-Value Matching Item: Pakistan	102
6.2	Use of National Assessment Findings to Improve Teacher Education: Minas Gerais, Brazil	106
6.3	Main Features of a Teacher In-Service Program Based on National Assessment Results: Uruguay	107
6.4	Poster Extract Published after National Assessment: Uganda	109
6.5	Mathematics Item	111
6.6	Recommendations Following a National Assessment in Mathematics, Grade 5: Ireland	114
6.7	Discussion Topics: National Assessment Results and School Effectiveness Variables	116
6.8	Discussion Topics: National Assessment Results and Teacher Effectiveness Variables	116
6.9	Discussion Topics: National Assessment Results and Individual Student and Family Factors Associated with Student Learning	117
7.1	Freedom of Information Laws	126
7.2	Agreements on the Release of National Assessment Results: Uruguay	127
7.3	Procedures to Maximize the Impact of National Assessment Findings	130
7.4	Brochure Cover for National Assessment, Ethiopia	133

FIGURES

2.1	Grade 4 Reading Skills and Strategies and Cut-Point Scores, by Benchmark Points, for the Combined Reading Literacy Scale, PIRLS, 2001	35
2.2	Percentages of Male and Female Students Achieving Mastery in National Assessment, Grade 4, by Curriculum Area: Sri Lanka	38
2.3	Percentages of Students Watching Television for Varying Amounts of Time, by Gender and Average Reading Score: Kuwait	38
2.4	Regional Differences in Achievement, Grade 4: Ethiopia	40
2.5	Mean Reading Test Scores of Students Plotted against Number of Books in the Home, Grades 1 and 5: Ireland	42

2.6	Trends in Average Reading Scale Scores for Students Ages 9, 13, and 17, NAEP, 1971–2004: United States	43
2.7	Mean Percent Correct Scores for Mathematics Content Strands in National Assessment, Grade 5, 1999 and 2004: Ireland	44
2.8	Mean Percent Correct Scores for Mathematics Skills in National Assessment, Grade 5, 1999 and 2004: Ireland	45
3.1	Average Reading Scale Scores by Race or Ethnicity, NAEP, Grade 4, 2005: United States	57
6.1	Reading Score Distributions of Pupils and Teachers: Vietnam	102
6.2	Grade 5 National Assessment in Mathematics in Vietnam: Correlation between Teacher and Pupil Provincial Mean Scores	105
6.3	Factors That Affect Achievement: Uganda	123

TABLES

1.1	Reasons for the Underuse of National Assessment Findings, Actions to Address Underuse, and Agents Responsible for Action	22
2.1	Mean Scores (and Standard Errors) of Boys and Girls in a National Assessment of Language and Mathematics	30
2.2	Mean Scores (and Standard Errors) and Scores at Varying Percentile Ranks in a National Assessment of Science, by Province	30
2.3	Mean Achievement Scores (and Standard Errors) in a National Assessment Administered at Two Points in Time	31
2.4	Correlation between Mean School Reading Achievement Scores and School Factors in a Grade 5 National Assessment	31
2.5	Percentages of Students Scoring at Minimum and Desired Levels of Mastery in Literacy, Numeracy, and Life Skills Tests: Mauritius	34
2.6	NAEP Mathematics Achievement Levels, Grade 4: United States	34
2.7	Grade 5 Reading Skill Levels in National Assessment: Vietnam	36
2.8	Mean Scores in Mathematics, Grade 8, by Racial Group, South Africa	39

2.9	Mean Scores in National Assessment of Nepali Language, Grade 5, by Region: Nepal	39
3.1	Technical Report: Suggested Contents	54
5.1	Percentages of Schools Possessing Selected Basic School Facilities: Kenya	81
5.2	Percentages of Schools Possessing School Facilities, 1990–2002: Malawi	82
5.3	Selected Countries That Used National Assessment Results in Reviewing the Education System	85
5.4	Ranking of Grade 4 Students Rated at or above Proficient on State and National Assessments, 2005: United States	89
6.1	Percentages of Students Whose Teachers Reported They Were Ready to Teach Mathematics, TIMSS Data, Grade 8	100
6.2	Percentage of Teachers Scoring at Each Mathematics Proficiency Level: Mozambique	103
6.3	Percentage of Students Answering Items Correctly in a Mathematics Assessment: British Columbia, Canada	110

FOREWORD

More than years of schooling, it is learning—or the acquisition of cognitive skills—that improves individual productivity and earnings, with gains for aggregate income in the economy. It has been shown, for example, that a one standard deviation increase in student scores on international assessments of literacy and mathematics competencies is associated with a 2 percent increase in annual growth rates of GDP per capita.

Measuring student learning outcomes is increasingly recognized as necessary, not only for monitoring a school system's success but also for improving education quality. Student achievement information can be used to inform a wide variety of education policies, including the design and implementation of programs to improve teaching and learning in classrooms, the identification of lagging students so that they can get the support they need, and the provision of appropriate technical assistance and training to low-performing teachers and schools.

The use of assessment results in order to improve student learning is a critical challenge for developing countries. Few of these countries measure student learning levels on a regular basis or in a systematic manner, and those that do tend not to use the results to inform their education policies. Yet better education policies have the potential to promote significant increases in cognitive skills. If developing countries are truly to achieve education for all, they will need assistance both with measuring their student learning levels and with finding ways to translate this information into effective education policies and practices.

This book will be a valuable support to those efforts. It brings together, for the first time, much of the existing research on what actually works in translating data from national assessments into actionable information and how to bring together stakeholders in conversations about this information in ways that will improve education quality and student learning. The book seeks to maximize an appreciation for the value of national data on student learning and to assist countries in fully exploiting the information that their assessments yield.

Elizabeth King
Director of Education
Human Development Network
World Bank

ACKNOWLEDGMENTS

A team led by Vincent Greaney (consultant, Human Development Network, Education Group, World Bank) and Thomas Kellaghan (Educational Research Centre, St. Patrick's College, Dublin) prepared the series of books titled *National Assessments of Educational Achievement*, of which this is the fifth volume. Other contributors to the series are Sylvia Acana (Uganda National Examinations Board), Prue Anderson (Australian Council for Educational Research), Fernando Cartwright (Canadian Council on Learning), Jean Dumais (Statistics Canada), Chris Freeman (Australian Council for Educational Research), Hew Gough (Statistics Canada), Sara Howie (University of Pretoria), George Morgan (Australian Council for Educational Research), T. Scott Murray (Statistics Canada and UNESCO Institute for Statistics), and Gerry Shiel (Educational Research Centre, St. Patrick's College, Dublin).

The work was carried out under the initial general direction of Ruth Kagia, director of education, her successor Elizabeth King, and Robin Horn, manager, Human Development Network, Education Group, at the World Bank. Robert Prouty initiated the project and managed it until August 2007. Marguerite Clarke managed the project in its later stages through review and publication. We are grateful for the contributions of the external reviewer, Al Beaton (Boston College). Additional helpful comments were provided by Patricia Arregui, Luis Benveniste, Marguerite Clarke, Shobana Sosale, and Emiliana Vegas. We received valuable input and support from David Harding, Aidan Mulkeen, and Myriam Waiser. Special thanks are extended to Hilary Walshe of the Educational Research Centre who typed the manuscript and to Mary Rohan who facilitated the work.

We thank the following people and organizations for permission to reproduce material in the text: Sylvia Acana, Martin Ackley, Abdulghani Al-Bazzaz, Aisha Al-Roudhan, Patricia Arregui, Educational and Developmental Service Centre (Kathmandu), Educational Research Centre (Dublin), Ethiopia Education Quality Assurance and Examinations Agency, Examinations Council of Lesotho, Lucien Finette, Zewdu Gebrekidan, Laura Gregory, Cynthia Guttman, Sarah Howie, International Association for the Evaluation of Educational Achievement, Tirth Khaniya, Mauritius Examination Syndicate, Claudia McLauchlan, Michigan State Board of Education, National Center for Education Statistics of the U.S. Department of Education, National Educational Research and Evaluation Centre (Colombo, Sri Lanka), Bob Prouty, United Nations Educational, Scientific and Cultural Organization (*EFA Global Monitoring Report*), Matseko C. Ramokoena, Rebecca Ross, Maureen Schafer, Bert Stoneberg, Sadia Tayyab, and Hans Wagemaker.

Book design, editing, and production were coordinated by Janet Sasser and Paola Scalabrin of the World Bank's Office of the Publisher. The Irish Educational Trust Fund, Bank Netherlands Partnership Program, Educational Research Centre (Dublin), and Australian Council for Educational Research generously supported the preparation and publication of the series.

ABBREVIATIONS

CONFEMEN	Conférence des Ministres de l'Education des Pays Ayant le Français en Partage
IEA	International Association for the Evaluation of Educational Achievement
MEAP	Michigan Educational Assessment Program
NAEP	U.S. National Assessment of Educational Progress
PASEC	Programme d'Analyse des Systèmes Educatifs de CONFEMEN
PIRLS	Progress in International Reading Literacy Study
PISA	Programme for International Student Assessment
SACMEQ	Southern and Eastern Africa Consortium for Monitoring Educational Quality
SIMCE	Sistema de Medición de la Calidad de la Educación (Chile)
TIMSS	Trends in International Mathematics and Science Study

CHAPTER 1

FACTORS AFFECTING THE USE AND NONUSE OF NATIONAL ASSESSMENT FINDINGS

The main objectives of a national assessment, as set out in volume 1 of this series, *Assessing National Achievement Levels in Education*, are to determine (a) how well students are learning in the education system (with reference to general expectations, aims of the curriculum, and preparation for further learning and for life); (b) whether there is evidence of particular strengths and weaknesses in students' knowledge and skills; (c) whether particular subgroups in the population perform poorly; (d) which factors are associated with student achievement; (e) whether government standards are being met in the provision of resources; and (f) whether the achievements of students change over time (Greaney and Kellaghan 2008). In pursuit of these objectives, through procedures established in the social sciences, data are collected from students and other stakeholders in the education system. Such data collection serves to make the outcomes of educational management and practice more transparent and has the ultimate purpose of providing personnel in the system with information designed to improve their practice (Ferrer 2006).

Evidence on the attainment of the objectives of a national assessment has implications for assessing important aspects of how an education system functions with respect to access, quality, efficiency, and equity (Braun and others 2006) (see box 1.1). The assessment will more than likely find that the issues are interrelated. In many education systems, low-achieving schools tend to serve students from disadvantaged backgrounds or a minority group; to receive the lowest level of resources (for example, textbooks may arrive late, if at all); and to have difficulty attracting teachers because of isolated location or for ethnic or language reasons. Clearly, any information that a national assessment can provide about these issues should be of interest to a wide range of stakeholders: politicians, education managers, teachers, teacher trainers, curriculum developers, parents, employers, and the general public.

Earlier books in this series described how information is obtained in a national assessment: how instruments to collect information on student achievement and associated variables are designed; how a sample of students is selected to represent the achievements of the education system as a whole (or a clearly defined part of it, such as grade 4 students or 11-year-olds); what procedures should be followed in collecting and cleaning data; and what methods may be used to analyze the data. This book turns to the reporting and use of data obtained in a national assessment with the ultimate objective of

---

BOX 1.1

Issues on Which a National Assessment Can Throw Light

Access. Obstacles to attending school, such as limited availability of places or distance of students' homes from school.

Quality. The quality of inputs to and outputs of schooling, such as the resources and facilities available to support learning (responsive curricula, teacher competence, textbooks); instructional practices; learner-teacher interactions; and student learning.

Efficiency. Optimal use of human and financial resources, reflected in pupil-teacher ratio, throughput of students, and grade repetition rates.

Equity. Provision of educational opportunities to students and attainment of parity of achievement for students, irrespective of their characteristics, such as gender, language or ethnic group membership, and geographic location.

Source: Authors based on Braun and others 2006.

improving the quality of students' learning. It is intended for two primary readerships: (a) those who have responsibility for preparing assessment reports and for communicating and disseminating findings and (b) users of those findings.

This introductory chapter addresses five topics. First, it describes aspects of the political context in which a national assessment is carried out and their implications for using assessment findings. Second, it discusses the issue of accountability, which is a major concern in many government administrations and one with which national assessment activities have been closely identified. Third, it notes that the quality of the instruments used in a national assessment to obtain information related to students' learning (the knowledge, skills, attitudes, and habits that students have acquired as a result of their schooling) has important implications for the use of findings to improve learning. Fourth, it considers how characteristics of a national assessment (census based, sample based, or international) affect the way findings can be used. Finally, it outlines possible reasons for the lack of use of national assessment findings.

THE POLITICAL CONTEXT OF A NATIONAL ASSESSMENT

Although one national assessment may look very much like another in many respects, there are, in fact, differences between assessments that have implications for use. Differences in design, implementation, and use arise from the fact that assessment is a political phenomenon (as well as a technical one), reflecting the agenda, tensions, institutional norms, and nature of power relations between political actors. Identifying the political context in which an assessment is carried out can help explain differences between countries in their evaluation strategies (Benveniste 2002). Even within the United States, accountability systems differ from state to state, reflecting administrative decisions and traditions that have evolved over time (Linn 2005b).

The role of assessment (and evaluation) in the exercise of control and power in educational matters has several facets. In the first place, assessment originates in a political process, often inspired and fashioned by political motivations. Second, the form of an assessment will be the result of competition among social actors who vie to influence the determination of norms and values that the state will privilege. Third, an assessment can affect social relations between, for example, education managers and teachers or teachers and parents. Fourth, control over the disposition and interpretation of assessment outcomes signifies authority to influence policy, resource allocation, and public perceptions. Finally, an assessment can involve mechanisms for regulation and for holding social actors accountable, implicitly or explicitly, for outcomes (Benveniste 2002).

The social actors with the ability to influence the nature of an assessment—and the ways findings are used—are many. How power politics actually play out in a country will depend on a number of factors, such as the following:

- The extent to which decisions regarding educational provision (for example, financing, curricula) are the function of central or decentralized governance
- The existence and strength of informal institutions, networks, and special interest groups, both within and outside government
- The strength of teachers' unions, which can play a key role in policy implementation, if not in policy formation
- The role of external (multilateral and bilateral) agencies in sensitizing administrations to address conditions in their education system and in providing or supporting development of the capacity to deal with them.

The implications of a political stance for a national assessment can be illustrated by two examples (Benveniste 2002). In Chile, emphasis is placed on accountability to the public, thereby promoting market competition, which is induced by publication of the results of an assessment for individual schools. Quite a different stance is represented in Uruguay, in which the state accepts responsibility for student achievement and for providing the resources required to support student learning—particularly that of the most underprivileged sectors of the population.

A further important aspect of the political context in which a national assessment is carried out that has implications for the use of findings is the extent to which an education system is open or closed. Some systems have been described as "exclusionary." In such systems, access to important information about aspects of the education system, including results of research, is limited to policy elites or senior decision makers, who do not permit public dissemination. At the other extreme, in more open systems, efforts will be made to attract the interest of the media, to mobilize political forces, and to generate debate about educational matters (Reimers 2003). An intermediate position relevant to the use of national assessment data is one in which the circulation of information about the education system, including student achievement data, while not totally restricted, is limited. For example, in Uruguay, student achievement data are intended primarily for consumption within the education community (Benveniste 2002).

ACCOUNTABILITY

Accountability movements, in response to political, social, and economic pressures, have in recent decades attained increasing importance in government administrations in many countries. This section considers accountability in the context of education and, in particular, focuses on the ways interpretation of the concept affects the use of national assessment data. It should be borne in mind that much of the discourse is based on experience in the United States and focuses on the accountability of schools (McDonnell 2005).

The development of accountability movements in the public sector (including education) can be related to a variety of factors that are not mutually exclusive, including the following:

- The need to manage finite (and in some cases decreasing) resources and to increase output for a given amount of input.
- The use of planning and management ideas that are borrowed from the business world, particularly ones relating to quality assurance, customer satisfaction, and continuous improvement (features of the New Public Management movement and a corporatist approach to administration). Such concepts may, in turn, involve defining

performance in terms of results, setting performance targets, using performance indicators to determine the extent to which targets are met, implementing strategic and operational planning, and basing resource allocation on performance.
- The introduction of market mechanisms of distribution and control involving incentive schemes, competition, contracting, and auditing, and the transfer of power relations into self-control mechanisms in an effort to minimize the need for external surveillance and to make individuals internalize the norms, values, and expectations of stakeholders and the mentality required to govern themselves.
- A movement toward more evidence-based practice. Such a movement requires data to support claims that individuals or institutions have performed professionally and efficiently, as well as data on which to base decisions regarding resource allocation (see Blalock 1999; Clegg and Clarke 2001; Davies 1999; Hopmann and Brinek 2007; Kellaghan and Madaus 2000).

A national assessment fits well with many of these factors by providing relatively simple statistical information (evidence) about the education system on a timely basis. Furthermore, it can identify subgroups or units in the population that meet a specified standard and ones that do not. The information can be used for planning and management—in particular, for deciding on the action required to improve quality or efficiency. It can also be used to hold social actors implicitly or explicitly accountable, thus placing on them the onus for change or adjustment.

The focus on accountability varies throughout the world, unfolding with different speeds and impact (Hopmann and Brinek 2007). It is thus not surprising that the purposes and goals of many national assessments—particularly in developing countries—or the ways such assessments fit into a system of accountability may not be very clear. In a situation in which accountability policies are not well developed, national assessment findings are unlikely to have much effect (Hopmann and Brinek 2007). However, at least an implicit recognition of accountability would seem to be necessary if use is to be made of assessment results. Otherwise, how are decisions to be made about the action that needs to be taken following an assessment and the individuals or institutions that will take the action?

Assigning accountability to the many stakeholders involved in a system as complex as education is not a trivial matter. Six questions that can help clarify the issues involved merit consideration in this task—particularly when national assessment results are used to hold schools and teachers accountable.

Should an Accountability System Focus on Outcomes?

A focus on the outcomes of education—in particular, student learning—can be attributed to the formal recognition and concern that many children spend a considerable amount of time in school without acquiring useful knowledge and skills. The need to ensure that children actually learn as a result of their educational experiences was highlighted at the World Conference on Education for All held in Jomtien, Thailand, in 1990 (UNESCO 1990) and again in the Dakar Framework for Action (UNESCO 2000).

To use data on the outcomes of education as the sole basis of accountability, however, is to lose sight of the fact that aspects of provision (for example, school buildings, curricula, educational materials, teachers' instructional techniques, and preparation activities) are also relevant in assessing quality. These factors are important if for no other reason than that the quality of student learning depends on them. Students "cannot be expected to become proficient unless and until the content and process of their classroom instruction well prepares them to do so" (Haertel and Herman 2005: 21).

Should an Accountability System Focus on Cognitive Outcomes?

Most people would probably agree that schooling has many purposes—some personal (for example, students' cognitive, moral, and social development) and some societal (for example, promoting social cohesion or nation building). Most would probably also agree that cognitive outcomes are preeminent and, moreover, that development of the literacy and numeracy skills measured in all national assessments is necessary as a foundation for students' later educational progress. It could hardly be considered satisfactory, however, if total reliance on these measures for accountability purposes were to result in the neglect of other valued outcomes of schooling related to attitudes, values, motivation, aspirations, self-concept, ability to work in groups, oral presentation skills, and socialization. Employers and economists have identified many of these outcomes (often described as *soft skills*) as very important in gaining employment (Cheng and Yip 2006).

Should an Accountability System Be Based on a Single Measure of Student Achievement?

In most national assessments, a single test (though it may have a number of forms) is used to assess students' competence in a curriculum area (for example, mathematics, reading, or science). Thus, a question arises: even if students' cognitive achievement is accepted as a legitimate criterion of the quality of schooling, is it reasonable to base the assessment of that quality (and a possible assigning of accountability) on a single measure of the performance of students at one or two grade levels?

The answer would seem to be no. A test can provide only a limited amount of information about student achievement (see box 1.2). An accurate picture of student learning, whether learning is being assessed at the national level or at the level of the individual school, requires multiple measures of achievement (Guilfoyle 2006).

If a test is limited to multiple-choice items, additional problems are likely to arise, because it is extremely difficult, using that format, to measure higher-level cognitive skills.

BOX 1.2

Evaluating Achievement on Limited Evidence

"Any system that hinges the evaluation of an entire school on one test score average from one group of students at one grade level cannot hope to accurately assess that school."

Source: Guilfoyle 2006: 13.

Should Sanctions Be Attached to Performance on a National Assessment?

A key decision in the use of national assessment findings is whether sanctions should be attached to student performance. Although some attribution of accountability, even if not explicitly acknowledged, might be expected after an assessment, it does not necessarily follow that sanctions will be applied. In some national assessments, however, sanctions are applied, usually to schools, teachers, and in some cases students. Examples of such instances can be found in the assessment of the national curriculum in England, which was introduced primarily as a tool of accountability, and in several state-level assessments in the United States. In such cases, an assessment becomes a high-stakes operation for schools, with a variety of rewards or punishments attached to student performance. Schools or teachers may receive rewards in the form of monetary bonuses, teachers may be dismissed, and students may be denied promotion or graduation.

A number of arguments support the attachment of high stakes to student performance on a test. First, it encourages individuals (in particular, teachers) to internalize the norms, values, and expectations of stakeholders (in particular, those of the ministry of education) and to accept responsibility for conforming to them. Second, it supports the operation of market mechanisms in the education system, involving competition, contracting, and auditing. Third, it serves to focus teacher and student endeavors on the goals of instruction and to provide standards of expected achievement that students and teachers can aspire to, thus creating a system of measurement-driven instruction. In this situation, one might reasonably expect student performance to improve if instruction has been closely aligned with an assessment instrument. Improved performance, however, may not be evident when student achievement is assessed on other instruments. When the achievement gains over time on the U.S. National Assessment of Educational Progress of students in states that have high stakes attached to their state-level assessments are compared with the gains of students in states that do not have high-stakes testing, the findings are ambiguous (Amrein and Berliner 2002; Braun 2004).

Arguments against attaching high stakes to students' test performance are based, for the most part, on observation and research on public examinations (rather than on national assessments) over a long period of time (Kellaghan and Greaney 1992; Madaus and Kellaghan 1992; Madaus, Russell, and Higgins 2009). Similar conclusions are emerging about the effects of testing associated with the No Child Left Behind legislation in the United States (Guilfoyle 2006). The available evidence indicates that when sanctions are attached to student performance, negative consequences follow:

- Teachers will tend to react by aligning their teaching to the knowledge and skills assessed in the test ("teaching to the test"), thus neglecting curriculum areas (for example, art, social studies, physical education) that are not assessed.
- Teaching will tend to emphasize rote memorization, routine drilling, and accumulation of factual knowledge, resulting in a passive approach to learning, rather than an approach that stresses higher-order general reasoning and problem-solving skills.
- Teachers are likely to spend considerable time developing students' test-taking strategies (such as how to answer multiple-choice questions) and may even use the multiple-choice format in their teaching (see box 1.3).

Should League Tables Be Published Following a National Assessment?

A particular example of the use of high stakes in a national assessment is the publication of results in the form of league tables in which

---

BOX 1.3

The Negative Effect of High-Stakes Accountability Uses

"Assessment systems that are useful monitors lose much of their dependability and credibility for that purpose when high stakes are attached to them. The unintended negative effects of the high-stakes accountability uses often outweigh the intended positive effects."

Source: Linn 2000: 14.

schools are ranked in the order of their performance. The expectation of this approach is that it will induce competition among schools and, in turn, improve student achievement (Reimers 2003). The information can be used to inform parents and communities, and in some situations, parents can use the information to make choices about schools for their children. Even when school choice is not an option or when parents do not use assessment results to make such a choice (Vegas and Petrow 2008), the mere publication of information about the performance of schools can pressure schools to improve their performance.

In addition to the adverse impacts on teaching and learning that have already been listed in relation to high-stakes assessment procedures, several other problems can be anticipated when results are calculated and published for individual schools (Clotfelter and Ladd 1996; Kane and Staiger 2002; Kellaghan and Greaney 2001; Linn 2000). First, the performance of schools (and thus their position in a league table) may vary depending on the outcome that is assessed (for example, reading or mathematics achievement). Second, even rankings that are based on the same measure can vary depending on the criterion of "success" that is used (for example, mean score or the proportion of students who obtain "high" scores). Third, the lack of precision in assessment procedures means that small differences between schools (which can have a large impact on their rank) will be due to chance. Fourth, achievement scores can vary from year to year because of factors that are outside the control of the school (for example, differences in cohorts of students). Small schools are particularly vulnerable to this problem. Fifth, the achievements of students in a school represent more than the efforts of teachers, as illustrated by the fact that school rankings based on achievement and socioeconomic data are almost identical (Vegas and Petrow 2008). Sixth, to take account of factors over which the school has no control (for example, student ability, home environment), the mean of gains in student test scores during a year may be used as the index of a school's performance. However, this measure tends to show very little between-school variance and has been therefore found unsatisfactory. Furthermore, it does not take into account the fact that the rate of students' growth is related to their initial achievements. More sophisticated statistical approaches, which take into account a range of factors over which schools do not have control, may be used in calculating school gain scores (value-added models). Problems that arise with these approaches are the complexity of the administrative procedures needed to collect the data, the level of statistical expertise required for analysis, the difficulties in the choice of variables to be included in statistical models, and the fact that adjustment for prior achievement may result in lower expectations for low-achieving students.

Finally, league tables invite corrupt practices, such as ensuring that low-achieving students do not take part in the assessment or focusing on the performance of borderline students to boost the mean score of a school. False information on conditions in schools may be provided (as occurred in Chile) to manipulate the socioeconomic categorization of the school if a low category attracts benefits.

Who Should Be Regarded as Accountable?

A major argument against attaching high stakes for schools and teachers to student performance in a national assessment is that an assessment does not identify the aspects of achievement that can be attributed to schools or teachers. Even a cursory reflection on the wide range of factors that interact to affect student performance should cause one to pause before assigning accountability. The factors can be identified as (a) characteristics of students, including their earlier achievements; (b) conditions in which students live, including family and community resources and support; (c) education policies and the resources and support, including curricula and teacher preparation, that are provided by the relevant public authorities; (d) school conditions and resources, including governance and management; and (e) competence of teachers (Kellaghan and Greaney 2001).

It seems reasonable to expect that the individuals or institutions associated with these factors should be held responsible and accountable only for the matters over which they have control. Thus, responsibility is shared by (a) students; (b) teachers; (c) schools; (d) policy makers, administrators, and managers of the school system (at national, state, regional, or municipal level, depending on how the education system is organized); (e) providers of support services (curriculum developers, teacher trainers, and textbook publishers); (f) parents; and (g) others (including politicians, taxpayers, and the society at large). In fact, it is extremely difficult to apportion accountability among this variety of stakeholders (see box 1.4). Failure to recognize this problem, however, may lead to incorrect attribution, which, in turn, may result in inappropriate action (see box 1.5).

BOX 1.4

Assigning Accountability for Student Achievement

Assigning accountability for student achievement is not easy:

- Although *teachers* are accountable to some degree for the achievements of their students, does this mean that they should be held solely accountable if the school in which they teach lacks basic amenities? If they have been inadequately trained? If students are absent for long periods? If the curriculum that they are required to teach is unsuitable for their students?

- Should *students* be held accountable if their homes do not value education or provide facilities or opportunities to study? If the curriculum is unsuitable? If their early educational experiences were marred by incompetent teaching?

- Should *parents* be held accountable if they do not send their children to school regularly because they cannot afford the costs involved or because they need the children to work?

- Should *education managers* be held accountable if they do not provide sufficient funds to meet the needs of schools?

- Should *politicians* be held accountable if the money available to government is inadequate to meet the demands of the education system?

Source: Authors.

BOX 1.5

Shifting the Blame for School Failure

"Accountability testing may subtly shift the blame for school failure from inadequate school resources, poor teacher preparation, or out-of-school factors to teachers and students who are 'simply not working hard enough,' and thereby divert attention from more costly, more needed reforms."

Source: Haertel and Herman 2005: 3.

Many national assessments, at least implicitly, recognize the role of factors outside the school in determining student achievement. Even in high-stakes assessments, test results are often presented separately for schools, depending on the socioeconomic status of the students whom they serve. Students' scores may also be adjusted to take account of the characteristics of students, such as prior achievements or the socioeconomic status of their families. Moreover, even when high stakes are attached, additional resources will usually be provided in schools experiencing difficulty. Such action accepts that teachers who are not performing well may need assistance and sustained professional development (Linn 2000).

A consideration of the variety of stakeholders that can affect students' learning supports the conclusion that assessing accountability is a complex matter and should not be based on the limited statistics that a national assessment provides. In the case of teachers, assessing accountability requires a clinical judgment that takes account of a range of factors, including the circumstances in which they teach. Such judgments are best made by a professional (a head teacher, inspector, or supervisor). Deciding on the accountability of other stakeholders is equally complex. Politicians are accountable to the electorate in a democratic system, but it is far from obvious what priority citizens give to education, much less to the achievements of students, when they cast their votes. Education managers are accountable to their superiors and political masters for the performance of their duties, but again it is not obvious whether student achievement should be a consideration. The remoteness of education managers from the actual work of the school, in contrast to the position of teachers, would probably ensure that student achievement does not play a role in assessing their performance.

Greater clarity and transparency about the responsibility and accountability of all individuals and institutions that contribute to the outcomes of the education system (including student learning) should serve to remove many of the ambiguities that exist in current accountability systems. Furthermore, use of an accountability system that includes all individuals, institutions, and agencies that exercise control over the resources and activities of schools should serve to focus the energies of all involved on performing the tasks for which they are responsible (Clegg and Clarke 2001).

THE QUALITY OF THE ASSESSMENT INSTRUMENT

The term *quality* applies to a variety of aspects of students' educational experiences, including learning environments that are safe and adequately resourced, curricula that are responsive to students' needs, instructional practices, competent teachers who engage in active pedagogies, and students' learning (see, for example, Schubert 2005; UNESCO 2000; UNICEF 2000). In national assessment studies, however, as we have seen, the major focus when considering quality is on cognitive outcomes of the educational process—that is, what students have learned—with a view to developing strategies to improve those outcomes. This emphasis is in keeping with target 6 of the Dakar Framework for Action, which highlights improving the quality of education "so that recognized and measurable learning outcomes are achieved by all, especially in literacy, numeracy, and essential life skills" (UNESCO 2000: 8).

In recognition of the central role accorded to student learning in a national assessment, this section describes four conditions that should be met to ensure (a) that the test that is used accurately represents the achievements that schools strive to develop and (b) that the information obtained serves the needs of users (Beaton and Johnson 1992).

First, because a test can measure only part of the knowledge and skills specified in a curriculum or a construct (for example, reading), ensuring that it provides an adequate representation of that knowledge and those skills is important (see Haertel and Herman 2005; Linn and Baker 1996; Messick 1989). Furthermore, test items should exhibit curricular importance, cognitive complexity, linguistic appropriateness, and meaningfulness for students. Hence, a test should not be limited to measuring isolated skill components or items of knowledge that require students only to recall facts or information (a feature of many national assessments) if the goal of the education system is to develop higher-level cognitive skills (involving reasoning, the ability to identify and solve problems, and the ability to perform nonroutine tasks). Test developers should have in mind the desirability of devising an instrument that will provide a basis for policy and decisions that are likely to induce curriculum and instructional changes that, in turn, foster the development of valued knowledge and skills (see Frederiksen and Collins 1989).

To secure adequate representation of a domain or construct—or of objectives or subdomains (for example, content strands or skills in mathematics)—a test should contain an adequate number of items. The small number of items in some national assessments must raise questions about their adequacy in this respect. For example, the number of items in tests in Latin American assessments (20–40, except in Brazil) means that content coverage has been poor. Furthermore, it is difficult to justify a view that mastery of a specific objective can be determined with only three or four items (González 2002). This sort of inadequacy is by no means limited to national assessments in Latin America.

Second, a test should assess knowledge and skills at a level that is appropriate for the students who will take it. A problem will arise if a test is based solely on curriculum documents if the curriculum contains unrealistic expectations for student achievement. In this situation, which is fairly common in developing countries, the test will be much too difficult for lower-achieving students and will fail to register their accomplishments. The solution lies in taking into account in test development not just the standards of the intended curriculum, but also what is known of the actual achievements of students in schools. In practical terms, very small proportions of students should get all the items right or all the items wrong. This result can be achieved by involving practicing teachers in the development and selection of test items and by carefully field-trialing items before the main assessment in a sample of students that spans the variation in schools of the target population.

A third condition that should be met if one is to be confident that a test provides valid information on students' knowledge and skills in a particular curriculum domain is that students' performance should not be determined by their competence in domains other than the one that the test was designed to assess (Messick 1989). For example, a test designed to assess students' achievement in science or mathematics should not contain so much language that performance on it depends on the differential ability of students to read rather than on their ability in science or mathematics. This problem occurs when it cannot be assumed that all students responding to the test possess the same level of skill in reading, which probably would be the case when the language of the test differs for some students from that which they normally use.

Finally, if assessment results are to be used to monitor change over time, the assessment instruments must be comparable. To achieve this result, the same test, which should be kept secure between administrations, may be used. If different tests are used, scaling with Item Response Theory allows results to be presented on the same proficiency scales (see volume 4 in this series). Best practice involves carrying a subset of items over from test to test to provide a strong means to link tests. It is also essential that student samples and the procedures followed in administration be equivalent. If exclusion criteria (for example, for students with learning difficulties) vary from one assessment to another, or if conditions over which administrators do not have control (for example, response rates) differ, such factors should be taken into account when comparisons are made between students' achievements at different points in time.

TYPE OF ASSESSMENT

The potential for use of the information derived from an assessment depends on the characteristics of the assessment. The use that can be made of assessment results varies for (a) *census-based assessments*, in which all (or most) schools and students in the target population participate (as, for example, in Brazil, Chile, and England); (b) *sample-based assessments*, in which a sample of students or schools that are selected to be representative of the total population take part (as is the practice in most countries); and (c) *international assessments*, in which a number of countries follow similar procedures to obtain information about student learning.

Census-Based Assessment

A national assessment in which all (or nearly all) schools and students, usually at specified grade or age levels, participate is termed *census* or *population based*. It has the potential to provide information on student achievement for (a) the education system in general, (b) sectors of the system, (c) schools, (d) teachers or classes, (e) individual students, and (f) factors associated with achievement. Because information is available about all schools, poorly performing schools can be identified, and decisions can be made about possible interventions, such as the provision of teacher professional development courses, supplementary services, or additional resources. The assessment will become high stakes if sanctions are attached to school performance or if information about the performance of individual schools is published.

Sample-Based Assessment

Because the whole population does not participate in a sample-based assessment, it can, unlike a census-based assessment, provide information only on student achievement for (a) the education system in general, (b) sectors of the system, and (c) factors associated with achievement. Although this focus limits the use that can be made of the assessment's findings, it has a number of advantages. First, a sample-based assessment is considerably less expensive to administer than is a census-based one. Second, it is not necessary to assess all students to meet the basic objective of a national assessment, which is to provide valid, reliable, and timely information on the operation of the education system and, in particular, on the quality of student learning. Third, because participating schools are not identified, a sample-based assessment does not have the negative impact on schools and learning of a census-based assessment if sanctions for schools, teachers, or both are attached to performance. Finally, sample-based assessments can be administered more frequently, thereby allowing successive assessments to focus on emerging issues. Some national assessments are administered on an ongoing basis to rolling samples of students, thus giving educators access to assessment data on a continuous basis.

International Assessment

Another distinction that is relevant in considering the use of assessment data is whether the assessment is a stand-alone operation or is carried out in the context of an international study. International studies hold the promise of providing information that is not obtainable in a national assessment. They can (a) help define what is achievable (how much students can learn and at what age) by observing performance across a range of education systems; (b) allow researchers to observe and characterize the consequences of different practices and policies; (c) bring to light concepts for understanding education that may have been overlooked in a country; and (d) help identify and question beliefs and assumptions that may be taken for granted (Chabbott and Elliott 2003). Furthermore, international studies tend to achieve much higher technical standards than do national assessments, and they allow participants to share development and implementation costs that might otherwise put these methods out of reach in many systems. The results of international assessments tend to attract considerable media attention and have been used to fuel debate about the adequacy of educational provision and student achievement, as well as to propose changes in curricula (particularly in mathematics and science) (Robitaille, Beaton, and Plomp 2000).

Although international assessments can—at least at a superficial level—provide comparative data on student achievement that are not available in a national assessment, caution is necessary when it comes to using the findings to inform domestic policy. Among the potential pitfalls in using international data for this purpose is that because a test has to be administered in several countries, its content may not adequately represent the curriculum of any individual participating country. It is also generally recognized that international studies do not pay sufficient attention to the contexts within which education systems operate. Indeed, it is unlikely that the technology that they use can represent the subtleties of education systems or provide a fundamental understanding of learning and how it is influenced by local cultural and contextual factors (Porter and Gamoran 2002; Watson 1999). If so, then one cannot assume that approaches identified in international studies that appear to work well in some education systems will be equally effective in others. Not only might the adoption and implementation of policies based on this assumption be ineffective but they could actually be harmful (Robertson 2005).

As well as providing comparisons between conditions in one's own education system and conditions in other systems, the data obtained in an international assessment may be used by an individual country to examine in-depth aspects of its own system (based on within-country analyses) in what becomes, in effect, a national assessment (Kuwait Ministry of Education 2008; Postlethwaite and Kellaghan 2008) (see box 1.6). Indeed, one of the aims of the International Association for the Evaluation of Educational Achievement 1990/91 Study of Reading Literacy was to provide national baseline data on the reading literacy of 9- and 14-year-olds for monitoring change over time (Elley 1992).

UNDERUSE OF NATIONAL ASSESSMENT FINDINGS

In considering the use of (and failure to use) national assessment findings, one must recognize at the outset that not a great deal of information is available about this topic. Furthermore, much less is

---

BOX 1.6

Two Uses of Data from an International Assessment

The distinction between the use of data collected in an international assessment for cross-national comparisons and that of data collected for national analysis may be illustrated by a comparison of the use of data collected in International Association for the Evaluation of Educational Achievement (IEA) studies in Hungary and Finland. In Hungary, the focus was on a comparison between its system of education and systems in other countries. The comparison indicated that (a) achievements in mathematics and science were satisfactory, (b) achievements in reading comprehension were generally inferior to achievements in other countries, (c) schools in Hungary were more diverse in their achievements than schools in other countries, and (d) home background had a greater influence on students' reading achievement in Hungary than in other countries (Báthory 1992). By contrast, in Finland, international data obtained in IEA studies were used to review the quality of mathematics and science education in the country. The data, which constituted the only empirical evidence available at the time on the achievements of students, were used in analyses that addressed particular needs and were fed to planners, policy makers, and ad hoc national working groups.

Source: Howie and Plomp 2005; Leimu 1992.

available about the optimal use of findings or about the effects of basing policy decisions on the findings. This lack of findings may not be a true reflection of actual use, of course, because information related to use by government bodies may not be publicly documented.

The evidence that is available indicates that the use of national assessment findings is not widespread, despite the potential that information derived from an assessment has for sparking reform and despite the expense incurred in obtaining such information. This observation has been made, for example, in the context of determining specific policies and decisions (see Arregui and McLauchlan 2005; Himmel 1996; Olivares 1996; Rojas and Esquivel 1998) and suggests that the use of national assessment data is very similar to the use of the findings of other policy-related research (see chapter 4). A description of the Honduran experience is probably typical of experience elsewhere (box 1.7). However, though identifying a specific use of assessment data might not have been possible in that case, the fact that the data influenced public opinion and raised consciousness is itself significant.

A variety of reasons may be advanced for the underuse of national assessment findings (table 1.1). First, findings are likely to be underused when the national assessment is considered to be a stand-alone activity, separate from and with little connection to other educational activity. This situation is likely to arise when national assessment

BOX 1.7

Extent of Use of National Assessment Results, Honduras

"These projects have produced a great amount of data and information describing students' educational achievement; they are research efforts which have a significant impact on public opinion but . . . have not contributed to make the educational system more efficient and effective. The results are scarcely used; they haven't been a real mechanism for control and accountability; and, to date, the information generated doesn't seem to have had meaningful consequences beyond informing, sensitizing, and raising consciousness."

Source: Moncada and others 2003: 73, as reported in Arregui and McLauchlan 2005: 6.

TABLE 1.1

Reasons for the Underuse of National Assessment Findings, Actions to Address Underuse, and Agents Responsible for Action

Reason	Action	Agent
1. National assessment activity regarded as a stand-alone activity, with little connection to other educational activities	Integrate assessment activity into existing structures, policy, and decision-making processes.	Ministry of education
2. Inadequate involvement of stakeholders in design and implementation of an assessment	Involve all relevant stakeholders in design and implementation of an assessment.	National assessment agency; ministry of education
3. Failure to communicate findings to all in a position to act	Make provision in the budget for dissemination, plan activities, and prepare a number of reports tailored to user needs.	National assessment agency
4. Lack of confidence in the findings of a national assessment	Ensure that the assessment team has the required technical competence and that relevant stakeholders are involved from the outset.	Ministry of education
5. Political sensitivity to making findings public	Increase the likelihood of making findings public by holding regular stakeholder discussions.	Ministry of education
6. Failure to devise appropriate action following an assessment at the level of general policies	Integrate national assessment activity into policy and managerial activities, and review findings to determine implications and strategies.	Ministry of education
7. Failure to devise appropriate action following a national assessment at the school level	Ensure adequate communication of findings to schools, review findings and devise strategies to improve student achievement, and provide ongoing support for implementation.	National assessment agency; ministry of education; schools and teachers; teacher trainers; curriculum authorities; textbook providers

Source: Authors' compilation.

activity is new or when it is carried out by external agents or at the request of donors. Rust (1999), for example, has pointed out that in Sub-Saharan Africa policy documents are often perceived by local bureaucrats as belonging to the donor agency and as separate from local policy making.

Second, underuse of national assessment findings is likely to occur when policy makers, education managers, and other stakeholders who are in a position to act on findings have had limited or no involvement in the design and implementation of an assessment.

Third, it is surprising, given the fact that assessments convey important information, that the first stage of use—the communication of information to relevant actors such as policy makers, providers of teacher training, and donors—is not always completed in a satisfactory manner, thus clearly limiting the potential for use. This problem may be due to a failure to budget for the dissemination of findings. In a situation in which most of the available project time and resources are required for the development and administration of instruments and analysis of data, nothing may have been left for the production and dissemination of information products and services.

Fourth, the deficiencies of many assessments in instrumentation, sampling, and analysis can raise questions about the validity of the data they provide, causing potential users to pause before acting on findings or to dismiss the findings altogether.

Fifth, if a national assessment identifies socioeconomic and educational inequalities associated with ethnic, racial, or religious group membership, this result may be a source of embarrassment to politicians, leading to attempts not to make findings public.

Sixth, appropriate policy and managerial decisions are unlikely to ensue from a national assessment if procedures and mechanisms are not in place (a) to consider the findings in the context of other policy and managerial activities and (b) to determine action on the basis of assessment findings.

Finally, national assessment findings are likely to remain underused unless all stakeholders who are in a position to act on findings (a) are adequately informed of the findings, (b) assess the implications of the assessment findings for their work, and (c) devise strategies designed to improve student learning. For example, in the case of schools and teachers, unless steps are taken to frame national assessment findings in a way that relates to teachers' concerns—and unless funds are provided to create mechanisms by which teachers can use the information derived from an assessment to guide reform—then the course of least resistance for school personnel may be at best to ignore the national assessment and at worst to undermine it.

These observations should serve to caution against having unrealistic expectations for the policy changes that can follow an assessment. Nevertheless, this book tries to show that assessment data can provide guidance to policy and decision makers by elaborating on the actions designed to address underuse that are listed in table 1.1. When possible it cites examples, garnered from a large number of countries, of actual use both to arouse public interest and in the initiatives of policy makers and managers. Less evidence is available about the critical and more complex area of use of national assessment findings in classrooms to improve student learning.

CONCLUSION

The use that can be made of the findings of a national assessment depends on a number of factors. The political context in which the assessment is carried out will have a strong bearing on use. Recognition that the assessment itself may be considered a political act reflecting the power, ideologies, and interests of social actors can serve to make the assessment—and decisions based on it—more transparent.

Because the instrument used to measure students' achievement is the cornerstone of a national assessment, its quality will affect the use that can be made of findings. For optimum use, test instruments should provide information about student achievements (a) that is accurate and comprehensive, (b) that measures a range of achievements, (c) that provides guidance for remedial action, and (d) that is sensitive to instructional change. The tests used in many national assessments do not meet these conditions. They may be limited to measuring lower-order levels of knowledge and skills, they may not contain a sufficient number of items, and they may be too difficult, with the result that potential users do not have a reliable basis for policy and decisions. The value of a national assessment for potential users will be enhanced if the background data on students' experience that are collected—and the procedures that are used to analyze data—point to factors that affect student learning and are amenable to policy manipulation.

A key decision for policy makers and education managers contemplating a national assessment that has implications for the use that can be made of findings is whether the assessment should be sample based or census based. A sample-based assessment will provide information and a basis for action at the system level, whereas a census-based one will, in addition, provide information about—and a basis for action in—individual schools. The choice of a sample-based or census-based assessment should be guided by a consideration both of the information needs of policy makers and managers and of the cost involved.

A census-based assessment provides the opportunity to hold schools accountable for student learning. Before deciding to use assessment findings for this purpose, policy makers should give serious consideration to (a) the limited information that a national assessment can provide about the quality of education provided by a school; (b) the range of individuals, institutions, and conditions that affect student learning; and (c) the negative (if unintended) consequences of attaching high stakes to student performance. Although an assessment used in this way as a mechanism of power may be corrective in the short term, in the longer term the bureaucratic imperative associated with it may corrupt the system that it was designed to correct or improve (Madaus and Kellaghan 1992).

When significant direct consequences are not attached to results, which is the case in most national assessments, the assessment is considered low stakes, and findings will be used primarily as a tool for planning and management (McDonnell 2005). The information that is obtained is considered to be a sufficient incentive for politicians, policy makers, educators, parents, and the public to act, and though the state may not accept responsibility for actual student achievement, it does accept its responsibility to make adequate provision for public education and to reduce disparities in the quality of education offered to—and achieved by—children of different ethnic backgrounds or social classes (Reimers 2003).

When a state adopts this position, detailed analysis of test results will be required to describe student achievements and to identify school and teacher practices that enhance those achievements. Following this, findings should be widely disseminated, resources and technical assistance should be provided to help schools identify problems they are experiencing, and continuing support should be provided for a process of school improvement.

This series of books has been written primarily to serve the needs of individuals carrying out a sample-based national assessment. However, the content of other volumes, except the module on sampling and some of the statistical analysis module, is also relevant to implementation of a census-based assessment. Much of the present volume is also relevant, though a number of issues are not (for example, identification of schools in need of assistance following a sample-based assessment). The prerequisites for effective use of the findings of a national assessment that will be considered are relevant to both sample- and census-based assessments and include the following:

- Involving policy and decision makers in the design of the assessment to address issues that they have identified as of pressing interest
- Communicating results in a timely fashion and in a form that is intelligible to key users
- Incorporating assessment information into existing bureaucratic structures and translating such information into policy, strategies, and policy instruments (for example, mandates, capacity-building strategies, inducements, and hortatory policies to motivate action)
- Ensuring that assessment findings influence the practice of classroom teachers, with the objective of improving student learning
- Providing continuing political support to use the findings to bring about change and to devise mechanisms that support their application in reform at the classroom level.

Throughout the volume, as the many activities that a national assessment can spawn are described, reference is made to census-based and international studies when they provide insights to use or when they describe practices that are relevant to a sample-based assessment.

Chapters 2 and 3 describe the types of reports that are needed to inform users of the findings of an assessment. Chapter 4 outlines general issues that merit consideration when translating assessment findings into policy and action. This chapter is followed by a description of specific uses of national assessment data for policy and educational management (chapter 5), for teaching (chapter 6), and to promote public awareness (chapter 7). The concluding chapter (chapter 8) identifies conditions that are likely to optimize use of the findings of a national assessment. It also suggests a number of ways in which national assessment activities could be modified and enhanced with a view to increasing their value to users.

CHAPTER 2

REPORTING A NATIONAL ASSESSMENT: THE MAIN REPORT

This chapter outlines the components of the main and essential instrument for reporting the findings of a national assessment. These components should include not only the findings but also the procedures followed throughout the assessment so that readers can judge their adequacy and relevance. The report will also form the basis of ancillary means of communicating the findings (for example, briefing notes, press releases, a report for schools—see chapter 3).

The main report of a national assessment should contain a description of the following components: (a) context of the assessment, (b) objectives of the assessment, (c) framework that guided the design of the assessment, (d) procedures followed, (e) descriptions of achievement in the national assessment, (f) correlates of achievement, and (g) changes in achievement over time (if appropriate data are available from a number of assessments). The amount of detail presented in the main report depends on whether a separate technical report is prepared. Most readers will have limited technical knowledge and are interested only in what the report implies for their work. Much of the technical detail can be assigned to the main report's appendixes.

At the outset, members of the national assessment team and key stakeholders should generally agree on how to design the main report, collect the data, and report the results. Reaching agreement about reporting results can be facilitated by drafting a series of blank or dummy tables and discussing the precise variables and data associated with each table. Table 2.1 is a blank table used to illustrate how national student-level data might be presented by curriculum area and gender. Table 2.2 suggests how provincial-level results might be presented to allow policy makers to compare levels of achievement among low-achieving students (those at the 5th percentile) and high-achieving students (those at the 95th percentile) in each province. Table 2.3 compares students' level of achievement at two points in time. Table 2.4 is designed to identify relationships between student achievement and a number of variables of interest to policy.

TABLE 2.1

Mean Scores (and Standard Errors) of Boys and Girls in a National Assessment of Language and Mathematics

	Language		Mathematics	
	Boys	Girls	Boys	Girls
Mean				
Standard error				

Source: Authors' representation.

TABLE 2.2

Mean Scores (and Standard Errors) and Scores at Varying Percentile Ranks in a National Assessment of Science, by Province

Province	Mean	Standard error	Percentile score			
			5th	25th	75th	95th
1						
2						
3						
4						
5						
6						
National						

Source: Authors' representation.
Note: These data can be used to prepare a box and whisker-type plots.

TABLE 2.3

Mean Achievement Scores (and Standard Errors) in a National Assessment Administered at Two Points in Time

First administration		Second administration		
Mean	Standard error	Mean	Standard error	Statistically significant?

Source: Authors' representation.
Note: One must take into account that both means are sample based in calculating the significance of the difference between them.

TABLE 2.4

Correlation between Mean School Reading Achievement Scores and School Factors in a Grade 5 National Assessment

Variables	r
Average class size, grade 5	
Average number of textbooks per student, grade 5	
Percentage of students who can be seated during writing class, grade 5	
Number of classroom teachers in school	
Number of registered students in school	
Number of years of teaching experience (grade 5 teachers)	
Level of teacher qualification (grade 5 teachers)	
Number of classroom resources	

Source: Authors' representation.

CONTEXT OF THE NATIONAL ASSESSMENT

In describing context, one may state the importance of obtaining information on student learning as a basis for policy and management decisions. A consideration of evidence from earlier studies on students' achievements (if available) will be relevant.

OBJECTIVES OF THE NATIONAL ASSESSMENT

The main objective should be stated: for example, to provide evidence on student learning in the education system. More specific objectives may also be stated: for example, to establish the current reading standards of fourth-grade pupils; to compare student achievements in private and public schools; to monitor trends in student learning over time; to describe school resources; to examine school, home background, and pupil factors that may be related to reading achievement; and to provide a basis for future assessments.

FRAMEWORK FOR THE NATIONAL ASSESSMENT

A framework is an overall plan or outline that describes what is being assessed in terms of knowledge, skills, and other attributes and how it is being assessed. The framework guides the development of the assessment and makes the assessment transparent, first, for those who construct the assessment instruments, but also for the wider audience who will read the report of the assessment. Chapter 2 in volume 2 in this series describes how to develop an assessment framework (Anderson and Morgan 2008).

The Progress in International Reading Literacy Study (PIRLS) provides an example of a description of the construct assessed in its study of the reading achievements of nine-year-olds (Mullis and others 2006; see also volume 1 of this series, Greaney and Kellaghan 2008: appendix B2). Reading is described in terms of two *purposes* (reading for literary experience and reading to acquire and use information) and four *processes* (focusing on and retrieving explicitly stated information, making straightforward inferences, interpreting and integrating ideas and information, and examining and evaluating content).

A framework also describes the instruments used to assess achievement. Including examples of the types of item used in the assessment is useful to provide readers with an idea of the nature of the tasks involved. Of course, these items should not include those planned for use in future assessments.

PROCEDURES IN ADMINISTRATION OF THE NATIONAL ASSESSMENT

How and when data were collected should be described. This description will include identification of the population on which the assessment was based, selection of schools or students for participation, and data on exclusions and nonparticipation.

DESCRIPTION OF ACHIEVEMENT IN THE NATIONAL ASSESSMENT

In deciding how to present the findings of a national assessment, it is important to bear in mind that the information provided should be relevant to policy makers' and decision makers' needs and should assist them in addressing policy problems constructively. The choice of a single index of student achievement (for example, a total mathematics score) or multiple indexes (for example, separate scores for computation and problem solving) may be relevant. Although policy makers may generally prefer summary statistics, reporting only a single index of achievement will most likely miss important information, thereby limiting the basis for action following the assessment (Kupermintz and others 1995).

Increasingly, a description of performance in terms of proficiency levels is being used to present the results of a national assessment. The procedure involves scale anchoring, which has two components: (a) a statistical component that identifies items that discriminate between successive points on the proficiency scale using specific item characteristics (for example, the proportions of successful responses to items at different score levels) and (b) a consensus component in which identified items are used by curriculum specialists to provide an interpretation of what groups of students at, or close to, the related points know and can do (Beaton and Allen 1992). The levels may be labeled (for example, satisfactory/unsatisfactory; minimum/desired; basic/proficient/advanced), and the proportion of students achieving at each level identified. Table 2.5 presents data from a national assessment in Mauritius.

Table 2.6, which describes levels of mathematics achievement in the U.S. National Assessment of Educational Progress (NAEP), goes beyond the type of data in table 2.5 in providing definitions of performance at a range of proficiency levels. The percentage of students (in public schools) at each level ranged from 44 percent at the basic level,

TABLE 2.5

Percentages of Students Scoring at Minimum and Desired Levels of Mastery in Literacy, Numeracy, and Life Skills Tests: Mauritius

Subject	Percentage of students	
	At or above minimal level	At or above desired level
Literacy	77.6	35.4
Numeracy	70.3	26.4
Life skills	71.6	32.4

Source: Mauritius Examinations Syndicate 2003. Reproduced with permission.

TABLE 2.6

NAEP Mathematics Achievement Levels, Grade 4: United States

Level	Expected achievement at grade 4
Basic	Students should show some evidence of understanding mathematics concepts and procedures in the five NAEP content areas. They should be able to estimate and use basic facts to perform simple computations with whole numbers, show some understanding of fractions and decimals, and solve some simple real-world problems in all NAEP content areas. They should be able to use, although not always accurately, four-function calculators, rulers, and geometric shapes. Their written responses will often be minimal and presented without supporting information.
Proficient	Students should consistently apply integrated procedural knowledge and conceptual understanding to problem solving in the five NAEP content areas. They should be able to use whole numbers to estimate, compute, and determine whether results are reasonable. They should have a conceptual understanding of fractions and decimals; be able to solve real-world problems in all NAEP content areas; and use four-function calculators, rulers, and geometric shapes appropriately. They should employ problem-solving strategies such as identifying and using appropriate information. Their written solutions should be organized and presented with both supporting information and explanations of how the solutions were achieved.
Advanced	Students should apply integrated procedural knowledge and conceptual understanding to complex and nonroutine real-world problem solving in the five NAEP content areas. They should be able to solve complex and nonroutine real-world problems in all NAEP content areas. They should display mastery in the use of four-function calculators, rulers, and geometric shapes. They are expected to draw logical conclusions and justify answers and solution processes by explaining why, as well as how, the solutions were achieved. They should go beyond the obvious in their interpretations and be able to communicate their thoughts clearly and concisely.

Source: U.S. National Center for Education Statistics 2006a.

to 30 percent at the proficient level, to 5 percent at the advanced level. Thus, 79 percent of students performed at or above the basic level (Perie, Grigg, and Dion 2005).

The approach to establishing proficiency levels differs in the 2001 PIRLS. Cut points were determined first by specifying the percentage of students in each benchmark category and then by examining the reading skills and strategies associated with each level (figure 2.1).

Vietnamese policy makers, working with other interested parties such as curriculum developers, identified six levels of student achievement in reading for grade 5 students using statistical information and the judgments of experts (table 2.7). Policy makers used the data to make national, provincial, and other comparisons of achievement.

In many national assessments, variance in student achievement is partitioned into between- and within-school components. This process involves calculating the intraclass correlation coefficient (rho), which is a measure of the homogeneity of student achievement within schools. It tells how much of the variation in achievement is between students within schools (within clusters) and how much is between schools (between clusters). A low intraclass coefficient means that

FIGURE 2.1

Grade 4 Reading Skills and Strategies and Cut-Point Scores, by Benchmark Points, for the Combined Reading Literacy Scale, PIRLS, 2001

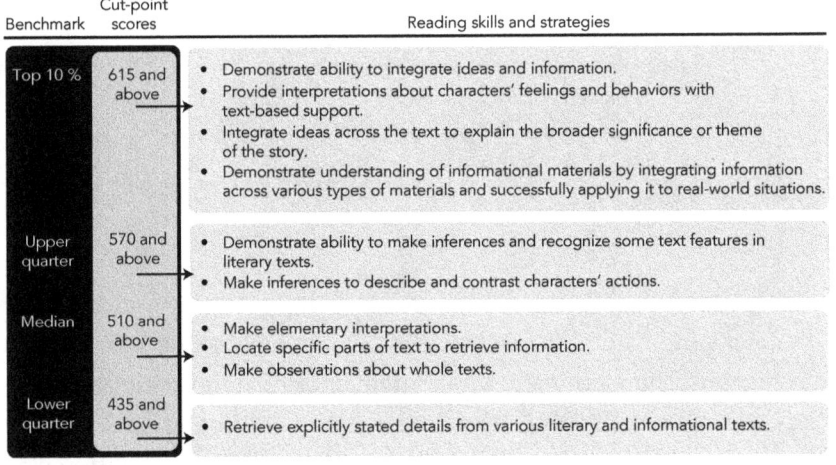

Source: Ogle and others 2003: figure 5.

TABLE 2.7

Grade 5 Reading Skill Levels in National Assessment: Vietnam

Skill level	Achievement	Percent of students	Standard error
1	Student matches text at word or sentence level, aided by pictures. Skill is restricted to a limited range of vocabulary linked to pictures.	4.6	0.17
2	Student locates text expressed in short, repetitive sentences and can deal with text unaided by pictures. Type of text is limited to short sentences and phrases with repetitive patterns.	14.4	0.28
3	Student reads and understands longer passages. Student can search backward or forward through text for information and understands paraphrasing. An expanding vocabulary enables understanding of sentences with some complex structure.	23.1	0.34
4	Student links information from different parts of the text. Student selects and connects text to derive and infer different possible meanings.	20.2	0.27
5	Student links inferences and identifies an author's intention from information stated in different ways, in different text types, and in documents where the message is not explicit.	24.5	0.39
6	Student combines text with outside knowledge to infer various meanings, including hidden meanings. Student identifies an author's purposes, attitudes, values, beliefs, motives, unstated assumptions, and arguments.	13.1	0.41

Source: World Bank 2004, vol. 2: table 2.1.

schools perform at comparable levels, while increasing values of the coefficient indicate increasing variation between schools in student achievement (Postlethwaite 1995). The findings of international studies (for example, PIRLS or the Programme for International Student Assessment, known as PISA) indicate that considerable differences exist between education systems in the value of the intraclass correlation. Furthermore, systems in which the national level of achievement is low tend to exhibit greater differences between schools in their achievement levels.

CORRELATES OF ACHIEVEMENT

A national assessment usually collects information on demographic and other background factors to allow comparisons to be made between the achievements of subgroups in the population. This information, when related in statistical analyses to student achievement, can answer questions that are central to the role of a national assessment, such as the following:

- Is the system underserving any particular group?
- Are gaps between groups in performance large enough to warrant remedial action?
- What factors are associated with low achievement?

In this way, by relating outcomes to inputs that are provided and processes being used, a national assessment shows "what is." However, it can also show "what might be" by demonstrating that some sectors in the system are achieving more desirable outcomes (high achievement) and by attempting to identify the factors associated with relative success.

If sample sizes in a national assessment are sufficiently large, evidence can be provided on achievement by gender; region (for example, province); location (urban or rural); membership of ethnic or language groups; and type of institution attended (public or private). Prompted in part by the current emphasis on gender equity in the Education for All and Fast Track Initiative programs, national assessments usually examine achievement differences between boys and girls. Figure 2.2 summarizes Sri Lanka's national assessment results for the percentages of male and female students achieving "mastery" in their first language, mathematics, and English.

A national assessment in Kuwait also identified gender differences in reading achievements (figure 2.3). In this case, gender differences were

FIGURE 2.2

Percentages of Male and Female Students Achieving Mastery in National Assessment, Grade 4, by Curriculum Area: Sri Lanka

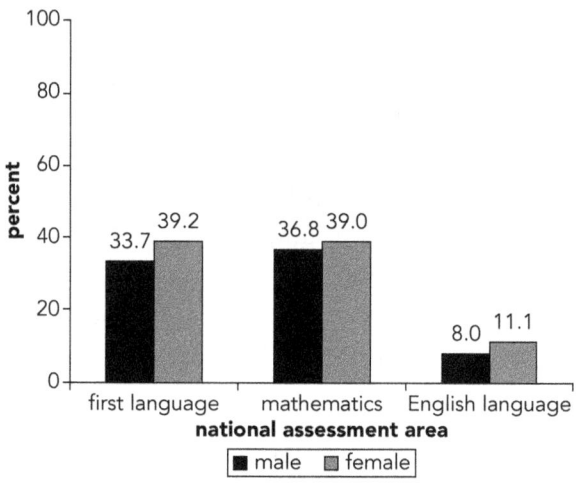

Source: Sri Lanka National Education Research and Evaluation Centre 2004: figure 4.44. Reproduced with permission.

FIGURE 2.3

Percentages of Students Watching Television for Varying Amounts of Time, by Gender and Average Reading Score: Kuwait

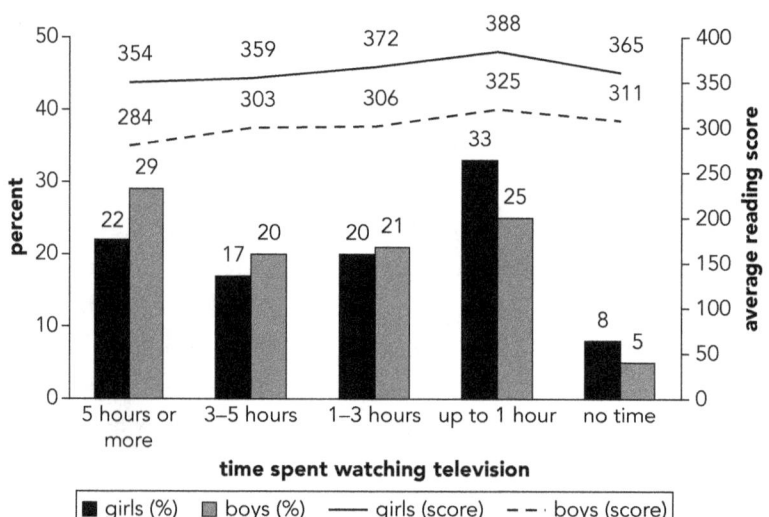

Source: Kuwait Ministry of Education 2008. Reproduced with permission.

associated with length of time watching television. Not surprisingly, perhaps, long periods spent watching television were associated with lower reading achievement scores.

Table 2.8 provides information on the mathematics achievements of racial groups in South Africa based on data collected for the Trends in International Mathematics and Science Study (TIMSS). Table 2.9 provides information on regional differences in a national assessment in Nepal.

Ethiopia's national assessment also provides information on the distribution of achievement by region (figure 2.4). Findings of the assessment suggest at least two policy options. They indicate, on the one

TABLE 2.8

Mean Scores in Mathematics, Grade 8, by Racial Group, South Africa

Racial group	Number of students	Mean score	Standard error	Minimum	Maximum
African	5,412	254	1.2	5	647
Asian	76	269	13.8	7	589
Colored	1,172	339	2.9	34	608
Indian	199	341	8.6	12	612
White	831	373	4.9	18	699
Total or overall mean[a]	8,147	275	6.89		
International mean		487	0.7		

Source: Howie 2002. Reproduced with permission.
a. Based on South African national data set for the Third International Mathematics and Science Study Repeat.

TABLE 2.9

Mean Scores in National Assessment of Nepali Language, Grade 5, by Region: Nepal

Region	Number	Mean scores	Standard deviation
Eastern	802	51.32	16.7
Central	932	50.91	19.5
Western	1,018	52.89	13.2
Midwestern	465	50.78	12.7
Far western	293	49.71	13.2

Source: Nepal Educational and Developmental Service Centre 1999. Reproduced with permission.

FIGURE 2.4

Regional Differences in Achievement, Grade 4: Ethiopia

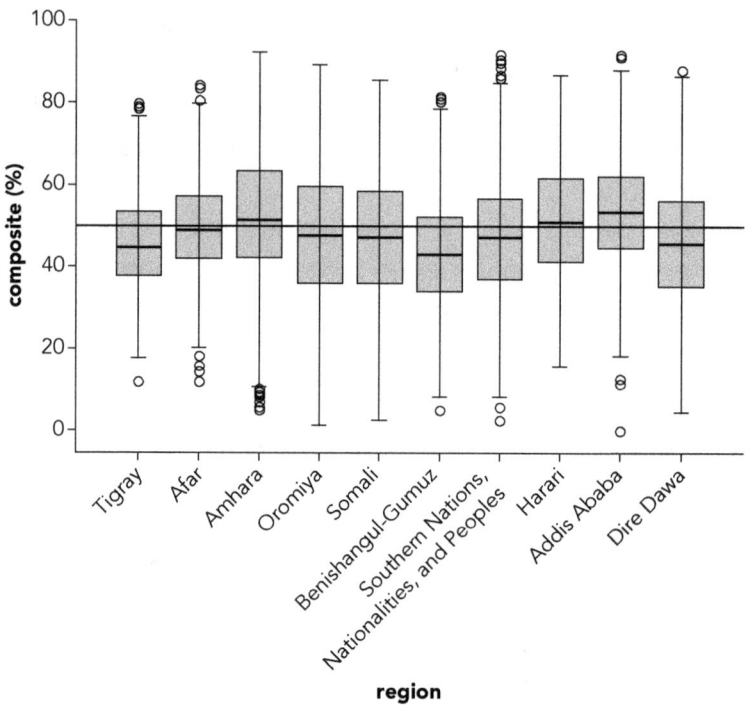

Source: Gebrekidan 2006. Reproduced with permission of the Ethiopia Quality Assurance and Examinations Agency.
Note: The mean is represented by the heavy black line; the box extends from −1 standard deviation (SD) to +1 SD, and the end lines from −1.96 SD to +1.96 SD. Markings outside the end lines represent outliers or extreme values.

hand, that support might be directed to the regions with the greatest number of low-scoring students (Oromiya, Somali, Dire Dawa) on a composite measure (based on scores on the reading, mathematics, environmental science, and English tests). On the other hand, the decision to provide support might be based on the lowest mean performance scores (Tigray, Benishangul-Gumuz).

Many (but not all) national assessments collect information in questionnaires about aspects of students' educational experiences and their home and community circumstances to provide clues about the school and extra-school factors that influence students' scholastic progress. In the Vietnam national assessment, for example, a private corner for study in a student's home was associated with higher achievement, even when more global assessments of home background were taken into account. High- and low-achieving schools and students could also be differentiated on the basis of regularity of meals and number of days absent from school (World Bank 2004).

Interpreting the findings of analyses in which student achievement is related to other variables requires some caution. A conclusion that factors related to student achievement may be considered to influence or "cause" achievement may not be warranted for a number of reasons, including the following:

- Causal interpretations of relationships identified in cross-sectional data can usually be sustained only if supported by other evidence.
- The number of schools or students in some categories may be too small to allow reliable inferences to be made.
- Methods of statistical analysis may be inappropriate. Analyses that explore relationships between two variables (for example, between class size and achievement) and that fail to take account of complex interactions in data (for example, between teacher qualifications and location of school) can lead to erroneous interpretations.
- Complex analyses are required to account for the influence on education outcomes of interacting factors operating at the student, school, and classroom levels. Because of this situation, multilevel, multivariate statistical techniques are required. These techniques isolate the effects of a variable that are net of the effects of other variables by systematically removing or adjusting for the effect of clusters of variables to show that significant differences exist or do not exist among students and schools after adjustment. For example, a conclusion that private schools are superior to public schools based on a finding that students attending private schools have higher levels of achievement than students attending public schools may not be supported when students' scores are adjusted to take account of their socioeconomic background.

Appreciation of the complexities involved in identifying causes of achievement will be strengthened by realizing that, more often than not, the background variables for which data are collected in a national assessment may only be proxies for factors that affect student learning

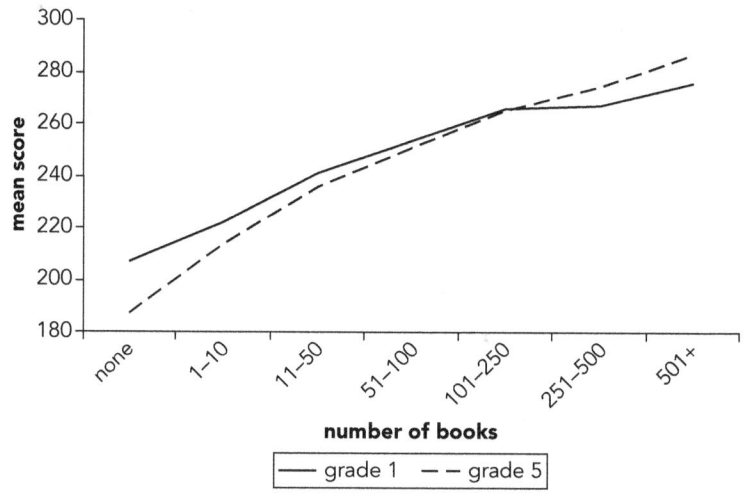

FIGURE 2.5

Mean Reading Test Scores of Students Plotted against Number of Books in the Home, Grades 1 and 5: Ireland

Source: Eivers and others 2005a: figure 4.2.

at a deeper level and in a more diffuse way. In that case, other research data need to be considered; even sophisticated statistical analyses may not be adequate. For example, although analysis might reveal a positive correlation between student learning and the number of books in a student's home (see figure 2.5), one would not be justified—even when other variables are taken into account—in concluding that number of books is causally related to student achievement. Although access to books may be important, student learning is likely affected not directly by the availability of books but by characteristics of an environment that cherishes books, such as one in which parents place a high value on scholastic achievement, provide academic guidance and support for children, stimulate children to explore and discuss ideas and events, and set high standards and expectations for school achievement (see Kellaghan and others 1993).

CHANGE IN ACHIEVEMENT OVER TIME

National assessments provide evidence of change in student achievement over time if assessment instruments are properly linked. When this information is available, findings may be presented as in the U.S. national assessment (NAEP) for the years 1971 to 2004 (figure 2.6). The plot of average reading-scale scores indicates that for students at age nine the average reading score was higher in 2004 than in any previous year. For students at age 13, the average score in 2004 was higher than the average score in 1971 and 1975, but no different from the average score in other years. Mean score in 2004 for students at age 17 showed a decrease from 1992. Volume 1 of this series (Greaney and Kellaghan 2008: 134) reported on changes in literacy scores over time in a number of African countries.

If assessment instruments permit (that is, if they provide adequate representation of curriculum subdomains), national assessments can provide evidence of change not just in gross measures of student achievement, but also in subdomains of a curriculum area. For example, the tests used in grade 5 national assessments in Ireland allowed

FIGURE 2.6

Trends in Average Reading Scale Scores for Students Ages 9, 13, and 17, NAEP, 1971–2004: United States

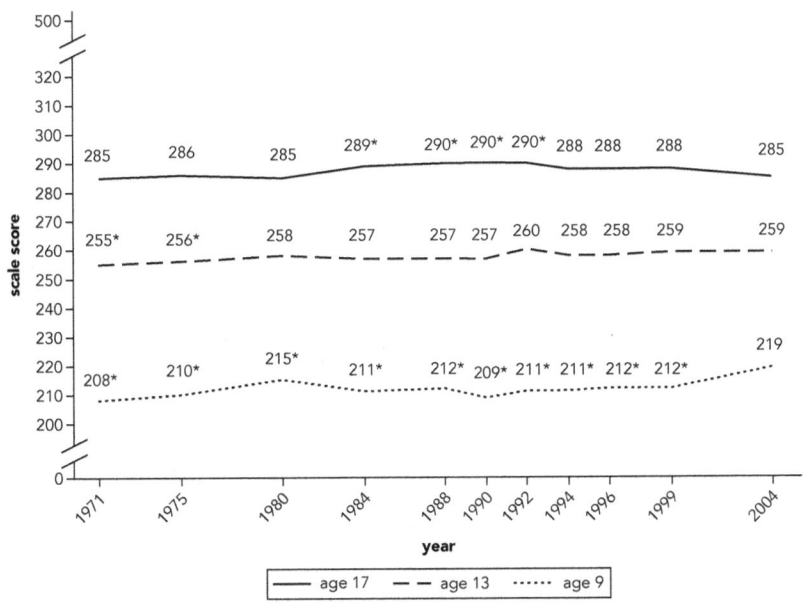

Source: U.S. National Center for Education Statistics 2005.
Note: *indicates that a score differs significantly from the score in 2004.

student performance to be estimated for a number of content strands and skills in mathematics. The results for assessments for five content strands, administered in 1999 and 2004, are presented in figure 2.7. The differences between years are statistically significant only for "shape and space" and "data and chance." In both cases, an improvement was registered between 1999 and 2004.

Data from the same national assessment are reported for five mathematics skill areas in figure 2.8. In this case, only the increase for "reasoning" was significant between 1999 and 2004.

In many countries, the need to monitor progress toward achieving the Millennium Development Goals of universal primary education by 2015 reinforces interest in assessing achievement over time. Efforts to improve the quality of education, however, may have to proceed in the face of problems created by expanding enrollments and decreased budgets. In Malawi, for example, performance deteriorated sharply following a campaign to provide schooling for everyone without providing the necessary resources to deal with the abolition of school fees and increasing numbers (Altinok 2008).

FIGURE 2.7

Mean Percent Correct Scores for Mathematics Content Strands in National Assessment, Grade 5, 1999 and 2004: Ireland

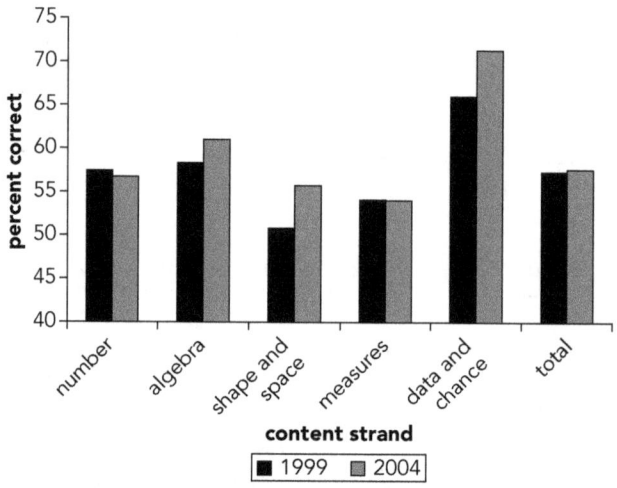

Source: Surgenor and others 2006: figure 3.1.

FIGURE 2.8

Mean Percent Correct Scores for Mathematics Skills in National Assessment, Grade 5, 1999 and 2004: Ireland

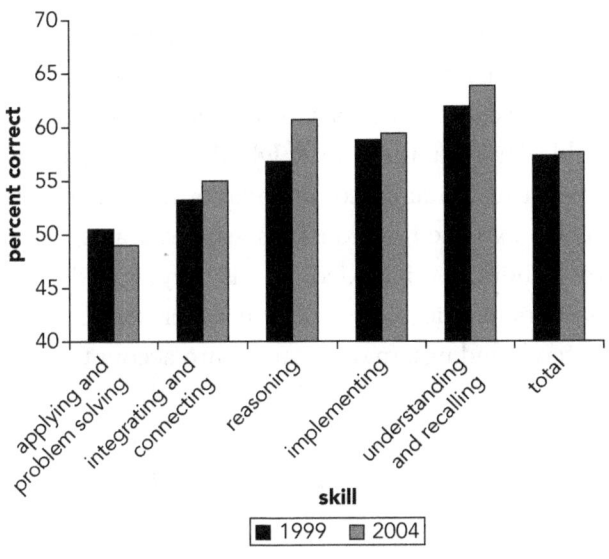

Source: Surgenor and others 2006: figure 3.2.

CONCLUSION

A main national assessment report should describe the study in sufficient detail to act as a primary source of information for the assessment. At the same time, it should not overload readers with inordinate amounts of technical information. Some reports do; others err in the opposite direction by providing inadequate information on technical aspects of the study, content of achievement tests, methods used, or error and bias in estimates.

Another error is to provide data only in tabular form. Because few potential users have the skills required to draw inferences from statistical tables, illustrating key findings in charts or graphs is a better method. Furthermore, a report that relies heavily on tabular presentation may fail to pay due attention to research findings that help explain relationships revealed in the assessment, such as why a variable (such as home background) is important and what is known about its influence on student achievement. This information, however, is critical if users are to appreciate the import of findings and are to be in a position to judge what action or actions may be required to address identified deficiencies.

Views and practices differ regarding the inclusion of recommendations in a national assessment report. Some national (and international) reports contain recommendations; others do not. National assessment teams should clarify at the outset whether a ministry of education expects a report to contain recommendations. Furthermore, if recommendations are expected, national assessment teams should ascertain whether they should be included only if they arise directly from the national assessment study or whether broader considerations, such as relevant research findings, may be taken into account.

CHAPTER 3

REPORTING A NATIONAL ASSESSMENT: OTHER INSTRUMENTS TO COMMUNICATE FINDINGS

In many cases, the only report issued following a national assessment is the type described in chapter 2. Because potential users of assessment data are numerous and different audiences have different requirements, this chapter describes additional ways of reporting findings that are tailored to meet a variety of needs. These methods range from publishing lengthy detailed reports to issuing short press releases and conducting individual briefings that summarize the main findings of an assessment. Although curriculum developers and textbook writers will require detailed information on student learning (more detailed perhaps than is available in a main report), a set of summary findings or highlights should be presented to citizens, who may have limited statistical acumen.

Pérez (2006) has identified the following general principles regarding the communication of research findings that can be considered applicable to national assessment findings:

- Use simple language, preferably in attractive media products such as videos.
- Clearly identify stakeholders, and tailor events and products to their needs.
- Consider recruiting public and credible leaders as advocates.

- Disseminate information to mass media. Events should be well advertised.
- Use slogans and simple messages that are readily understood. For example, a statement such as "an eight-year-old child should be able to read a 60-word story in one minute and answer three questions about its content" illustrates what a standard means.
- Back up all broadcast or large-audience dissemination materials (including PowerPoint presentations) with supporting technical information.

The procedures and instruments that a national assessment team may use in addition to the main report are described in this chapter and include the following: briefing ministerial and senior policy personnel; preparing briefing notes; publishing summary reports, technical reports, and thematic reports; securing media reports; issuing press releases; holding press conferences; conducting individual briefings; posting Web site reports; and making assessment data available.

PRODUCT SPECIFICATION SHEET

The manager of a national assessment will find preparing a product specification sheet useful in planning the preparation of reports. The sheet should include the following elements:

- Product name (for example, main report)
- Summary description of the product
- Intended users
- Product priority
- Detailed product description
- Key production activities, responsibilities, and time schedule
- Production costs
- Projected release date (and venue if appropriate)
- Product price
- Dependence on other products or inputs.

Because the potential number of products and services will almost inevitably outstrip the technical and financial resources available to the national assessment team, products should be prioritized so that those with the greatest potential for instituting reform will be produced. The national assessment team should plan and cost the full spectrum of products and services, however, to allow the team to move rapidly if additional funding becomes available.

BRIEFING MINISTERS AND SENIOR POLICY PERSONNEL

National assessment teams should prepare briefings (most likely in written form) for the minister and senior officials in the ministry of education. They will want information that captures the main findings of an assessment in a concise form and the possible implications of those findings (Beaton and Johnson 1992). Because ministers tend to get numerous documents to read on a daily basis, a briefing note must be short and to the point.

Ministers and their senior officials are rarely interested in reading full reports, but they do need to be aware of key findings and to be alerted to issues that the media, parliament, or stakeholders in the education system (for example, teachers' unions) may raise when the report of an assessment is published. They need this information even if the news is "bad." For some audiences "good" news is not always welcome because it can imply that additional resources are not needed.

Particular attention needs to be paid to how differential outcomes for subpopulations are reported and interpreted. If some groups perform poorly, it can be politically embarrassing for politicians because the results can be interpreted as evidence of neglect of those segments of the population. It may even be a reason for not holding a national assessment at all or, if one is held, not publicizing the results.

Many government ministries have standard formats for ministerial briefings. These formats should be used unless they are considered inadequate for the task. Effective briefing notes on a national assessment might include the following:

- Concisely stated purpose for carrying out the assessment
- One or two sentences on why it is important for the minister to know the results
- Brief description of the background of the assessment (such as who did it and what target population was assessed)

- Key results, especially those that might have policy implications (such as student achievement levels, regional and gender differences, resource allocation to schools)
- Possible next steps that might present options, such as discussing whether the minister should make a public statement about some of the results, recommending study of the results by a curriculum authority or by teacher training institutions, or suggesting a further national assessment in a different curriculum area
- Recommendations to advise the minister on a response to be taken to the listed options
- Information on whether attachments are included, such as a press release, a summary of the national assessment, or the complete report
- Name of the national assessment team member to be contacted in case the minister requires additional information.

PUBLISHING SUMMARY REPORTS

A summary report for nontechnical readerships is often published in addition to a main report. The summary report can be very brief, as is the case of the state-level summaries or snapshots provided by the U.S. National Assessment of Educational Progress (NAEP) on its Web site. Box 3.1 presents the summary report for the performance of fourth-grade students in Illinois on the 2007 reading assessment.

Some summary reports may be longer. For example, following a national assessment of geography at grades 4, 8, and 12, the National Center for Education Statistics produced a summary of the results in the NAEP facts series (approximately six pages), under the title "Geography: What Do Students Know and What Can They Do?" The report described what students at the 25th, 50th, and 90th percentiles at each grade level had mastered (Vanneman 1996). Other reports are lengthier and may include a brief description of all the components of the main report.

Main and summary reports are available for the national assessment of English reading in Ireland (Eivers and others 2005a, 2005b). Both publications can be accessed on the Educational Research Centre Web

> **BOX 3.1**
>
> **Summary Report of Illinois State Grade 4 Students' Reading Achievement Levels on the 2007 NAEP: United States**
>
> [State snapshot report from the Nation's Report Card, *Reading 2007*, Illinois Grade 4 Public Schools (NCES 2007-497IL4). The report includes sections on Overall Reading Results for Illinois; Percentages at NAEP Achievement Levels and Average Score; Performance of NAEP Reporting Groups in Illinois: 2007; Average Score Gaps Between Selected Groups; and Reading Scores at Selected Percentiles.]
>
> *Source:* U.S. National Center for Education Statistics 2007.

site (http://www.erc.ie). The main report of the U.S. NAEP for history (grades 4, 8, and 12) and a summary report can be downloaded from http://nces.ed.gov/nationsreportcard/ushistory/.

Classroom teachers are often the primary readership for summary reports. In that case, summary reports are likely to include recommendations for teaching that arise from the assessment (see chapter 6). For example, a teacher's guide to the mathematics achievements of Irish 15-year-olds was published following the administration of the

Programme for International Student Assessment (PISA) test in Ireland in 2003 (Shiel and others 2007). The report contains examples of test items along with information on student performance and on the extent to which Irish teachers teach PISA-type mathematics. Box 3.2 contains three of a number of recommendations for teachers that are in the report.

Summary reports may focus on other interest groups, as follows:

- Teachers' unions represent the collective interests of teachers and can be powerful agents for—or against—change. They often have a strong vested interest in using information to support their positions.

BOX 3.2

Suggestions for Applying the PISA Approach to Teaching and Learning Mathematics: Ireland

The following recommendations are from a teacher's guide that was prepared by the Educational Research Centre and was published by the Irish Department of Education and Science following a national assessment:

> Emphasise a more interactive approach to teaching mathematics, in which students are engaged in discussing problems, both before they are solved, and afterwards. Discussion should focus on identifying the mathematics needed to solve a problem, and on communicating students' reasoning after it has been solved.
>
> Emphasise the full range of cognitive competencies (processes) during teaching. The overemphasis on reproduction in classrooms and in examinations means that many students may not get an opportunity to apply higher-level competencies such as Connecting and Reflecting. It is likely that the application of these competencies by students at all levels of ability will result in greater conceptual understanding and more independence in solving problems.
>
> Implement a better balance of context-free questions and questions that are embedded in real-world contexts. Many of the questions in current textbooks and examination papers are context-free. While such items play an important role in developing basic mathematics skills, it is also important to provide students with opportunities to engage with real-world problems. Such engagement serves to make mathematics more relevant for them, and provides them with opportunities for developing a broader range of mathematical competencies.

Source: Shiel and others 2007: 48.

- Community leaders, including local politicians, need information to determine if the education system is producing what the community needs to achieve social, cultural, and economic goals.
- Employers and business leaders need objective information about student learning achievements as an indicator of the quality of preparation of future employees.
- Citizens may use information from a national assessment to judge whether the education system is meeting its goals with reference to access, quality, efficiency, and equity, which may lead to pressure to improve education provision.
- Donor agencies seek objective information to evaluate program effectiveness or to justify assistance to the education sector or to a particular population subgroup or geographic region.

PUBLISHING TECHNICAL REPORTS

Technical reports are a crucial element of a national assessment because they provide members of the research and scientific communities with detailed information about the assessment that allows them to evaluate it critically. Technical reports also act as a record of the activities involved in the assessment, which is needed to implement future cycles of an assessment.

Some national assessments publish only one report, which serves as both a general and a technical report. The Australian report for students' achievement in information and communication technologies in years 6 to 10 is an example; it contains technical details on proficiency levels and sampling procedures (Ainley, Fraillon, and Freeman 2007).

Other reports focus on the more technical aspects of sampling, item analysis, scoring techniques and criteria, scaling, statistical analyses, and quality control. Examples can be found in *The Trends in International Mathematics and Science Study 2003: Technical Report* (Martin, Mullis, and Chrostowski 2004) and in *Reading Literacy in the United States: Technical Report of the U.S. Component of the IEA Reading Literacy Study* (Binkley and Rust 1994).

Table 3.1 lists activities that a technical report should cover. Particular attention should be paid to instrument development, a description

TABLE 3.1
Technical Report: Suggested Contents

Section	Some activities	Examples or comments
Purpose	Describe the context and the major objectives of the national assessment.	Monitor changes in achievement levels since the last national assessment, report on regional differences in student achievement, or both.
Definition of subject	Define the subject being assessed. List aspects of the subject being assessed (such as vocabulary, comprehension, behavior).	Reading literacy is defined as the "ability to understand and use those written language forms required by society and/or valued by the individual" (Campbell and others 2001: 3).
Details of what is being measured	Describe content areas and cognitive levels to be assessed for each subject and grade level. Include item details.	Include a blueprint or table of specifications. Indicate the number of multiple-choice, close-constructed-response, and extended-response items.
Instrument development	Give details of construction of pilot tests, questionnaires, and administrative manual, including revisions.	Include a summary of curriculum authority and teachers' reviews of appropriateness of test items. If tests or questionnaires were translated, describe how the accuracy of translation was checked.
Population or sample assessed	If a sample, indicate sample size and criteria for excluding students, grouping schools, and replacing schools.	Report on the desired, defined, and excluded population (for example, age or grade, public and private); participation rates; sample stratification; type of sample (for example, cluster, number of stages); method of determining sample size; and method of calculating error.
Operations	Describe selection of administrators and quality control measures.	Describe procedures for ensuring safe delivery, storage, and return of all assessment instruments.

Scoring	Describe scoring procedures and quality control measures.	Indicate percentage of different types of test items that were subject to independent rescoring.
Data entry and cleaning	Describe procedures and quality control measures.	Explain how specific errors in student records were identified and changed.
Item analysis	Summarize item difficulty and discrimination levels.	Indicate whether items were technically adequate across regions and linguistic groups, if applicable. Give reasons for any item deletion.
Item scaling	If using item response theory, explain how scale scores and proficiency levels were computed.	Describe the role of subject matter specialists in determining proficiency levels.
Analysis of assessment data	Present summary statistical results, including standard errors. Compare results with those of earlier national assessment, if appropriate. Analyze data on issues suggested by steering committee.	List precise statistical procedures; identify software used; describe method of calculating standard errors, levels of statistical significance, and ways missing data were handled. Explain how indexes (for example, school resources, parental interest in education), if used, were calculated. Compare regional differences in achievement. Relate achievement to characteristics of student (age, gender, attitudes toward subject); school (teacher qualifications, school resources); or home background (family size, parental education).
Conclusions	Give summary of main findings. Advise on limitations of the results.	Give justifiable recommendations based on the results if requested at the outset to do so.

Source: Authors' compilation.

of the population or sample that was assessed, item scaling, and statistical analysis.

PUBLISHING THEMATIC REPORTS

Thematic reports explore aspects of the findings of an assessment related to a specific theme that are not addressed in detail in the main report. A thematic report could analyze error patterns in students' responses to particular aspects of the curriculum or to sets of items in an achievement test. Such analyses can help identify where a curriculum needs to be reformed or instruction needs to be strengthened. For example, an analysis of error patterns in 2006 PISA science items was conducted for Qatari students (DataAngel Policy Research 2007). Despite its potential to improve practice, very little analysis of this type is undertaken.

A thematic report can focus on a subpopulation that is of interest to a particular audience or that relates to a particular policy (for example, boys and girls, race or ethnicity groups, students in disadvantaged backgrounds, rural students). Figure 3.1 provides an example that compares the reading achievement scores of students, who are classified by race or ethnicity on the basis of national assessment data in the United States.

Examples of thematic reports that incorporate advanced statistical methods and present results in an accessible, policy-relevant way can be found in studies using data from the Southern and Eastern Africa Consortium for Monitoring Educational Quality, or SACMEQ, and the Programme d'Analyse des Systèmes Educatifs de la CONFEMEN (Conférence des Ministres de l'Education des Pays Ayant le Français en Partage), or PASEC, on the cost-effectiveness of school inputs (Michaelowa and Wechtler 2006) and rural-urban literacy differences (Zhang 2006) and studies using PISA data on 15-year-olds' "engagement in reading" (Kirsch and others 2002).

SECURING MEDIA REPORTS

Paper-based products in the form of reports are expensive to produce. Besides, this kind of publication may not be appropriate for many

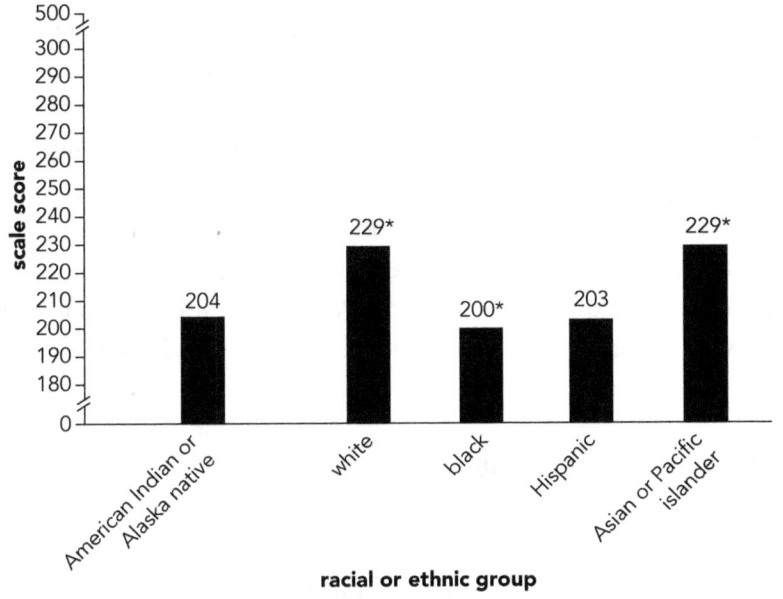

Average Reading Scale Scores by Race or Ethnicity, NAEP, Grade 4, 2005: United States

Source: U.S. National Center for Education Statistics 2006b: figure 2.17.
Note: Results are based on the national NAEP sample. *Black* includes African American; *Hispanic* includes Latino; and *Pacific islander* includes Native Hawaiian. Race categories exclude Hispanic origin. * indicates that the score is significantly different from that of American Indian and Alaska Native students.

individuals who might have an interest in the findings of a national assessment. In contrast, the media—print, radio, television, or videos—can provide an inexpensive way of disseminating the main messages of a national assessment to individuals who probably would not otherwise learn about them. On the one hand, failure to get media coverage may mean that an assessment goes largely unnoticed. On the other hand, when the media are critical of an assessment—or create sensational or inaccurate messages—the national assessment system may be threatened.

Radio can reach large numbers of individuals and may be particularly appropriate for individuals with low literacy skills. Television, too, can reach large numbers and has an important role in arousing public interest. However, radio and television presentations are usually too superficial and short to provide any real understanding of the findings of a research study or of their implications.

A more in-depth use of television to inform the public of the results of an assessment was achieved in Latin America. Following the release of the results of an international assessment carried out by the Laboratorio Latinoamericano de Evaluación de la Calidad de la Educación (see volume 1, appendix C3, of this series—Greaney and Kellaghan 2008), details were publicized through a video shown on television throughout the continent (Ferrer and Arregui 2003). The case for using videos and television to report the findings of a national or international assessment is strengthened by the finding in Peru that videos were much more effective than lectures or PowerPoint presentations in dialogue with stakeholders on educational policy (Pérez 2006).

ISSUING PRESS RELEASES

A press release is a short written statement issued to the media. The format and content will vary depending on who issues it. A press release from the ministry of education will tend to highlight the positive aspects of findings, whereas one issued by a research body will tend to take a more neutral stance. At the outset, the person responsible for drafting the press release should clarify the type of audience being targeted. Audiences can include the general public, government officials, or experts. Knowing the audience will help determine the amount of technical information to include and the tone of the press release.

Preparing a press release helps reduce, but does not eliminate, the tendency of reporters to oversimplify assessment findings. Some reporters may strive to highlight a politically damaging finding instead of presenting a neutral, balanced view.

A press release should start with the date of release and the name and address of the agency (ministry of education, research institute, or other agency) responsible for the release. If possible, the agency's logo should appear in the heading. The heading should be presented in boldface type and should be short and interesting; it may be the only chance of attracting the reader's attention. "National Assessment Report Released" is short, but "New Report Highlights Successes in Education Sector" is both short and interesting. An initial or lead sentence to arouse the reader's interest, followed by one or two sentences that elaborate on the lead, should be written.

The main section of a press release should be factual and should contain brief answers to the following questions:

- Who carried out the national assessment?
- Why was it carried out?
- When was it carried out?
- How was it carried it?
- What were the main findings?
- Why are they important?

Drafters of a press release should do the following:

- Have a clear idea of what they expect readers to conclude from the press release
- Confine themselves to the facts and not embellish the findings
- Avoid long sentences, technical terms, and statistical jargon
- Use active-voice verbs
- Phrase the text as they would like it to appear in the newspaper
- Limit the release to one, or at most two, double-spaced pages
- Check to see that the text is factually and grammatically correct and free from spelling errors
- Provide a contact phone number, as well as postal and e-mail addresses
- Use ### under the last line of text to signify the end of the press release.

If diagrams are used, they should be easily understood, have a clear purpose, and not attempt to present too much detail or use footnotes. Graphs in the form of bars, rather than lines, are considered more effective (Hambleton and Slater 1997).

Box 3.3 presents an excerpt from the two-page press release on the 2007 national assessment in the United States. Another sample news release is provided in box 3.4.

BOX 3.3

Press Release Excerpt, NAEP: United States

NEWS RELEASE

Embargoed, Hold for Release until Tuesday, Sept. 25, 10 a.m. EDT
CONTACT: Matt Maurer, (202) 955-9450 ext. 322,
mmaurer@communicationworks.com
U.S. Students Show Progress in Math and Reading,
According to 2007 Nation's Report Card™
Minority Students Post Some of the Larger Gains

WASHINGTON (September 25, 2007)—Overall, student achievement in mathematics and reading in the United States is on the rise, according to results from The 2007 Nation's Report Card™, with some of the larger gains made by the nation's minority students.

Two reports released today, *The Nation's Report Card™: Mathematics 2007* and *The Nation's Report Card™: Reading 2007*, detail the achievement of 4th- and 8th-graders on the National Assessment of Educational Progress (NAEP), administered by the U.S. Department of Education earlier this year. The reports compare national and state data in 2007 with each prior year the tests were given, beginning in 1990 for mathematics and 1992 for reading. Based on national averages, mathematics scores for 4th- and 8th-graders have continued to rise since 1990. In addition, the proportion of students performing at or above the *Basic* and *Proficient* achievement levels has increased markedly over the last 17 years. Gains made since 2003 are statistically significant, although not as large as those realized during some earlier periods. Meanwhile, the average reading score for 4th-graders was the highest in 15 years and has increased since 2003, though the overall gains since 1992 have been more modest than those seen in mathematics. The average 8th-grade reading score has improved slightly since 2005 but remains below the level of achievement shown in 2002 and is about the same as the average in 1998.

...

Copies of *The Nation's Report Card™: Mathematics 2007* and *The Nation's Report Card™: Reading 2007*, plus extensive information from the 2007 NAEP mathematics and reading assessments, will be available online at http://nationsreportcard.gov at 10 a.m. EDT on September 25.

#

(continued)

BOX 3.3

The Nation's Report Card is the only nationally representative, continuing evaluation of the condition of education in the United States and has served as a national yardstick of student achievement since 1969. Through the National Assessment of Educational Progress (NAEP), The Nation's Report Card informs the public about what America's students know and can do in various subject areas, and compares achievement data between states and various student demographic groups.

Source: http://www.nationsreportcard.gov/math_2007/media/pdf/newsrelease.pdf.

BOX 3.4

Sample News Release: United States

This sample press release was published by the Michigan State Board of Education in "Pencils Down: A Guide for Using and Reporting Test Results":
FOR IMMEDIATE RELEASE:
DATE:
CONTACT:
Public Relations Officer
Mary Green
555-1313

    Mathville Schools Cite Late Coverage as Possible Cause for Small Gain in Test Scores

    Mathville fourth-, seventh-, and tenth-grade students showed only slight improvement in some areas tested on the Michigan Educational Assessment Program (MEAP) test taken in late September.

    In a report to the Mathville Board of Education, Superintendent Phred Smart said that "although we are pleased to see some improvement, much work needs to be done, especially in the area of math." Although Mathville students tested above the state average in a few areas, Smart said, "We are reviewing our math program in light of the fact that many of the concepts tested are not taught to our students prior to the testing date."

    ___ percent of the Mathville fourth-graders, ___ percent of the seventh-graders, and ___ percent of the tenth-graders attained three-quarters of the objectives at each level.

    Smart indicates that seventh-grade math will receive considerable study by a district math study committee. The math study committee is composed of first- through ninth-grade teachers, the school district math consultant, and the building principal.

(continued)

BOX 3.4

___ percent of the fourth-grade readers at Mathville accomplished three-quarters of the reading objectives compared with ___ percent of the students on a statewide basis.

Seventh-graders scored higher than the state average on ___ of the 25 reading objectives tested with ___ percent of the students mastering at least three-quarters of the objectives as compared to ___ of the students on a statewide basis. ___ percent of the tenth-graders attained three-quarters of the reading objectives compared with ___ percent of the students on a statewide basis.

The MEAP is given to every fourth-, seventh-, and tenth-grader in Michigan's public schools each fall. This testing has been required under Michigan law since 1969. The test is used by teachers to design programs to meet special learning needs of students.

The MEAP helped to determine whether students have learned specific skills in reading and math. Test questions are taken from a pool of questions considered to reflect the basic skills considered critical by Michigan educators.

Copies of the district's assessment results are available to the public at the district administrative offices, 242 13th Street.

Source: Gucwa and Mastie 1989. Reproduced with permission of Michigan State Board of Education.

HOLDING PRESS CONFERENCES

If the intent is to reach a wide range of the media, including press, radio, and television, holding a press conference is generally necessary. Key members of the national steering committee (if possible) and the national research coordinator should present the findings. Presentations should take about 20 minutes, and about another 10 minutes should follow for questions. Because experience suggests that keeping speakers from straying from agreed messages can be difficult, speakers should practice their presentation in advance, as well as their responses to expected questions.

Participants should receive a copy of a press release, a summary report of the national assessment results, brief biographical notes about the speakers, and a background note on the agency that conducted the assessment (if other than the ministry of education).

Press conferences to promote the dissemination of national assessment results can involve risk. Some journalists and interest groups may have an interest in sensationalizing the results and in misrepresenting key messages. Media questions often focus on poor results. The popular media in many countries have a tendency to provide simplistic explanations of complex issues (such as causes for falling or rising standards of student achievement). It is important that the press conference be used to correct unwarranted conclusions, such as laying the blame for poor results on a single cause or group (for example, teachers, ministry of education, or textbooks).

CONDUCTING INDIVIDUAL BRIEFINGS

Often, publicizing the central message from a national assessment is more effectively done by meeting separately with individuals rather than by holding a press conference. Individual media events can help the national assessment spokesperson establish a rapport with a journalist or with a radio or television reporter. Such events also allow time to clarify possible misconceptions.

POSTING WEB SITE REPORTS

In the future, increasing access to the Web site will help ensure that more people have access to national assessment results. Chile publishes detailed results on its national assessment Web site (http://www.simce.cl). The Irish Department of Education and Science presents summary findings of national assessments on its official Web site (http://www.education.ie/servlet/blobservlet/des_cos_preface.htm). The opening page of the site for mathematics achievement simply lists the chapter headings of the report, each of which can be downloaded by clicking (box 3.5). The U.S. NAEP Web site goes further by permitting interested educators and members of the public to seek answers to specific questions by carrying out their own comparative analysis of the data (box 3.6). By logging on to the Web site (http://nces.ed.gov/nationsreportcard), individuals with little or no statistical competence can obtain answers to questions related to performance in their own state, such as the following:

> **BOX 3.5**
>
> **Web Site, Mathematics Achievement in Primary Schools: Ireland**
>
> The Web site of the Irish Department of Education lists the contents of the national assessment report on mathematics achievements. Users can simply click on the following titles to see the report:
> - Preface
> - Chapter 1—The Context of the Assessment
> - Chapter 2—Assessment Instruments and Procedures
> - Chapter 3—Mathematics Achievement of Pupils in Fourth Class
> - Chapter 4—Pupil Characteristics and Mathematics Achievement
> - Chapter 5—Home Background and Mathematics Achievement
> - Chapter 6—Classroom Environment and Mathematics Achievement
> - Chapter 7—School Characteristics and Mathematics Achievement
> - Chapter 8—Learning Support for Mathematics
> - Chapter 9—Inspectors' Views on Teaching and Learning Mathematics
> - Chapter 10—Recommendations
> - Appendices
> - Glossary
>
> Source: http://www.education.ie/servlet/blobservlet/des_cos_preface.htm.

- Have standards gone up or down since the last NAEP?
- Are there gender differences in reading achievement?
- How do minority students compare to the overall state average in reading?
- How do state scores compare with those of neighboring states or with the national average in science?

MAKING ASSESSMENT DATA AVAILABLE

Actual assessment data are an often-neglected asset; however, a variety of agencies or individuals might have an interest in carrying out secondary analyses of the data. They include officials from ministries other than the education ministry (for example, health, civil works, or finance); researchers; faculties of educational institutions; and donor agencies seeking an objective justification for supporting national or

BOX 3.6

Site Map, NAEP Web Site: United States

| SAMPLE QUESTIONS | ANALYZE DATA | STATE PROFILES | PUBLICATIONS | search NAEP |

THE NATION'S REPORT CARD

National Assessment of Educational Progress (home)

Site Map

About NAEP	NAEP Subjects	Special Tools
Overview	The Arts	NAEP Questions Tools
FAQs	Civics	NAEP Data Explorer
NAEP Activities	Economics	State Comparisons
Information for Selected Schools	Foreign Language	State Profiles
Parents' Information	Geography	
Inclusion of SD/ELL Students	Mathematics	
National NAEP	Reading	**More Resources**
State NAEP	Science	Contact Us
Urban District NAEP (TUDA)	U.S. History	Publications
Long-Term Trend NAEP	Writing	Glossary of Terms
High School Transcript Study	World History	Assessment Schedule
National Indian Education Study		NewsFlash Service
Special Studies		No Child Left Behind
NAEP Partners		Technical Documentation
National Assessment Governing Board		Research e-Center
		Background Questionnaires
		Sample Questions Booklets
		Stat*Chat* (Archive)

Source: U.S. National Center for Education Statistics 2008.

targeted interventions. Barriers to use by individuals or agencies other than the national assessment team, while largely technical, include issues of privacy and confidentiality.

The traditional method of satisfying the needs of secondary users has been to produce and publish huge volumes of statistical tables. These publications, however, are difficult to use, and the tables they contain often do not meet the exact needs of the user. Commercial products such as iVision allow large volumes of preplanned tables to be accessed readily.

Many national assessments choose to produce for users a microdata file and associated technical documentation that have been screened to protect the confidentiality of individual students, teachers, and schools. Where users require access to student data, national teams may set up a remote access service to which external users submit an analysis code that is run on the confidential database. The results are then vetted for confidentiality. Although somewhat cumbersome, this method allows national study teams to protect confidentiality—an important consideration given that participation often depends on guarantees that results for individual schools, teachers, or pupils will not be made public.

National study teams may need to convince politicians and ministry officials that making national assessment data accessible is in their long-term interests, even if it might cause some short-term pain by putting data in the hands of potential critics.

OTHER DISSEMINATION INSTRUMENTS

Other instruments used to disseminate the findings of a national assessment include conferences, workshops, seminars, newsletters, and brochures focused on particular groups of stakeholders (for example, ministry officials or teachers).

Conferences, workshops, and seminars provide mechanisms to advertise the availability of assessment results to key stakeholders in a variety of ways. They provide the opportunity to reach consensus on the meaning of key findings and on the steps that need to be taken to remedy any identified problems. These methods are particularly appropriate to inform the following groups:

- Curriculum developers, who can find information in a national assessment that identifies weaknesses in student achievement that have implications for curriculum revision
- Textbook writers, who, as in the case of curriculum developers, may need to revise textbooks and supporting materials (for example, teacher manuals) in light of evidence on student achievement revealed in a national assessment
- Teacher trainers (preservice and in service), who may use the findings of a national assessment to identify areas of weakness in teacher preparation or in teachers' pedagogical practices.

CONCLUSION

Many countries adopt a number of approaches to disseminate the findings of a national assessment. For example, in Colombia, results were released through the mass media, and a program of national and local workshops was organized to discuss results and their implications. Strategies for improving educational quality were discussed at a national seminar, and local administrators and individual teachers were sent information on national and regional results in newsletters and brochures. In Ireland, wide coverage of an assessment was achieved through a general report, a summary report (aimed primarily at teachers), and a press release. The results were also reported on radio and television and in newspapers, and a national seminar in which administrators, teachers, and academics participated was organized jointly by the ministry of education and the agency responsible for implementing the national assessment (Educational Research Centre).

Many national assessment authorities do not adequately communicate assessment findings to the variety of individuals and bodies that have a legitimate interest in knowing about student learning in schools. This deficiency inevitably places severe limitations on the use of findings. Various reasons may account for this situation, including lack of interest on the part of senior ministry officials, lack of development of an infrastructure surrounding national assessment activities, lack of appreciation of the role that a variety of stakeholders can play in responding to national assessment findings, and lack of resources to produce several reports and to operate a variety of information channels geared to the needs of potential users.

As national assessment systems mature, many demands will be made on the limited resources available for an assessment. These demands will be related to frequency of assessment, improvement of the technical quality of assessments, upgrading of the skills of personnel who carry out assessments, and enhancement of the capacity of policy makers and education managers to absorb and use the information obtained in an assessment. In this situation, hard choices will have to be made about the optimal allocation of resources. In making these choices, one must not overlook the importance of procedures to optimize use by communicating findings in an appropriate form to interested parties.

CHAPTER 4

TRANSLATING ASSESSMENT FINDINGS INTO POLICY AND ACTION

Although the primary purpose of a system of national assessment is to describe students' learning, its role is not limited to description. To justify the effort and expenditure involved, the information that an assessment provides about the achievements of students, their strengths and weaknesses, and how they are distributed in the population (for example, by gender or location) should be useful in informing policy and making decisions (related, for example, to resource allocation). A national assessment is also envisaged as providing information to curriculum developers, textbook writers, teacher trainers, and the public. In this view, an assessment should provide more than information; following dissemination, it should become a lever of reform.

This chapter outlines five topics that are relevant when considering how assessment information might be translated into policy and action: (a) institutional capacity to absorb and use information, (b) trustworthiness and relevance of the information provided by the assessment, (c) procedures to identify appropriate policy or action following an assessment, (d) determination of a systemwide or targeted intervention, and (e) complexity of policy formation and decision making. The focus is primarily on institutional arrangements in the education system. Later chapters address more specific uses of a national assessment for policy and educational management (chapter 5) and for teaching (chapter 6).

INSTITUTIONAL CAPACITY TO ABSORB AND USE INFORMATION

A number of conditions relating to institutional capacity should be met if optimal use is to be made of the findings of a national assessment (Kellaghan and Greaney 2004; Postlethwaite 1987; Vegas and Petrow 2008). First, political will, openness to new information, and readiness to consider change or reform on the part of policy makers are particularly important. Second, policy and decision makers in the ministry of education should have the capacity (knowledge and skills) to interpret and use information from a national assessment. Considerable investment may be required to develop this capacity, particularly in countries in which national assessment activity is new. Third, a national assessment should not be seen as an isolated activity. Rather, it should be integrated into existing structures, policy-making and decision-making processes, and channels of resource allocation.

Fourth, the national assessment team should ensure that systems and strategies are in place to communicate its findings to institutions and agents who will have a role in implementing policy (for example, local administration structures; supervisors, inspectors, and advisers; curriculum development authorities; schools; and teachers). Fifth, after their capacity has been developed, the continuity of staff members in organizing and undertaking assessments and in interpreting findings must be ensured. Turnover of officials and technical experts, which is a common occurrence in many developing countries, will have a negative impact on capacity. Finally, the support and commitment of all stakeholders is required. Hence, the purpose, findings, and implications of the national assessment should be clearly communicated, and the concerns of stakeholders who may feel threatened by policy or decisions should be addressed.

TRUSTWORTHINESS AND RELEVANCE OF INFORMATION PROVIDED BY AN ASSESSMENT

Before considering what decisions they might base on the findings of a national assessment, decision makers should satisfy themselves that the information provided by the assessment is trustworthy and realistic. This conclusion will be warranted (a) if the national assessment team is technically competent, (b) if the knowledge and skills of students that the test was designed to measure are adequately represented in the assessment instrument, (c) if proper procedures have been followed in the collection and analysis of data, and (d) if student learning is described in appropriate detail and in a way that is sensitive to the needs and technical expertise of users (chapter 1; see also Postlethwaite 2004a: chapter 5).

Policy makers and managers require information that addresses their issues of concern and that provides a basis for their policy formation, planning, and decision making. Many examples exist of national assessments failing to meet this need. For example, if the test used in an assessment is too difficult and fails to discriminate at lower levels of achievement, the assessment will not provide the information that a senior ministry official needs to make decisions about resource allocation for low-achieving students. Assessment results that provide only mean scores or a ranking of geographic regions based on such scores without an analysis of the achievement that the scores represent will not provide sufficiently detailed information for curriculum developers and teacher trainers. Finally, assessment reports that take three or four years to complete are unlikely to be of much interest to policy makers because the findings may no longer be relevant to the issues or to the personnel who prompted the assessment.

PROCEDURES TO IDENTIFY APPROPRIATE POLICY OR ACTION FOLLOWING AN ASSESSMENT

In some cases, the findings of a national assessment will point directly to action needed to address an identified problem. More often than not, however, the action required will not be obvious. The assessment will identify problems, but the information it provides will not generate a solution or select among alternative courses of action. For example, the assessment may provide evidence that students perform poorly in some achievement domains, or it may identify relationships between achievement and background factors, indicating that girls' achievement is inferior to boys' achievement or that students in small rural schools perform less well than students in urban schools. However, the identification of factors related to student achievement does not provide any obvious explanation why the genders or students in different locations should differ in their achievements. Many national assessments address this issue to some extent when they collect additional data on the conditions in which learning takes place. The results of analyses in which these conditions are related to student achievement, although not identifying specific courses of action, can lead to greater understanding of the factors that affect outcomes and provide a basis for policy formation and decisions (Blalock 1999).

Apart from recognizing the complexity of reaching decisions following an assessment, policy and decision makers have to be cognizant of the feasibility and cost-effectiveness of follow-on initiatives or reforms. Clearly, priority should be given to the identification of inputs that are likely to make a difference to learning. Thus, while some inputs (for example, an elaborate school facility) might be highly attractive, they might not be more effective than more modest inputs. The impact of the cost of an intervention on the education budget is also relevant. Although students might learn better in very small classes, the cost of implementing a small-class strategy in developing countries may be too high to be considered a viable option (Lockheed and Verspoor 1991).

This chapter identifies four (not mutually exclusive) procedures in which assessment findings can play a role in suggesting appropriate policy or action following an assessment.

Discussing the Findings

The most important activity following a national assessment is involving stakeholders in a discussion and interpretation of its findings to try to tease out its implications, to suggest causal relationships, and to propose approaches for addressing identified problems. A variety of sources of information and expertise and many stakeholders have a role to play in interpreting the findings and searching for solutions. The contribution of individuals who are in close contact with the day-to-day operation of schools (teachers, inspectors, supervisors, or advisers) will be particularly important.

Many countries hold seminars and workshops following a national assessment to allow a variety of viewpoints to be heard. Other, more formal approaches to reviewing findings (for example, in the deliberations of a national commission or in devising a national sector strategy) are also used (see chapter 5).

Letting the Findings "Enlighten" the Policy-Making Process

Use of the findings of other policy-oriented educational research suggests that the impact of national assessment findings would be conceptual rather than instrumental. Thus, findings would enter the policy arena, not through the direct application of results, but in the way of generalizations, orientations, and general guidance that "enlighten" the policy-making process, shaping the way that people think about issues and informing general debate and discussion (Husén 1984; Weiss 1979). In this view, research use is a gradual and diffuse process, providing concepts and theoretical perspectives that permeate the policy-making process, affecting understanding of educational issues, and suggesting appropriate solutions to problems.

"Enlightenment" should not be restricted to policy and decision makers. Making public the results of a national assessment can raise consciousness not just among policy makers and managers but also among citizens in general. Raising public awareness, in turn, can serve to underline the important role that education plays in meeting national goals and harness public opinion to support efforts to improve provision.

Although the advantages of enlightenment may be obvious, using research findings in this way can have disadvantages. First, the process is open to oversimplification and distortion. Second, poor research may attract as much attention as good research. Third, some important research findings may never reach policy or decision makers. Although use of national assessment findings to enlighten stakeholders (including the public) about the state of the education system is to be encouraged, more is required. The ministry of education and other key stakeholders should study carefully the findings of a national assessment so that they can devise specific policies and actions to address identified deficiencies.

Responding to Specific Problems Identified in a National Assessment

In some national assessments, the action required to address specific problems will be obvious. For example, if schools are found not to have resources specified in ministry regulations (for example, textbooks), steps will need to be taken to provide those resources. If teachers' knowledge of subject matter is inadequate, in-service courses targeted on identified weaknesses would seem the most obvious way to remedy the situation.

Referring to Other Research Findings

A consideration of other research findings can help strengthen the basis for drawing inferences regarding causal relationships that a national assessment might suggest, providing a more secure basis for policy formation. These findings could arise from a variety of studies, including studies of school and teacher effectiveness; studies of the relative influence of school and home factors on student learning; and studies of classroom processes, of class size, and of the effects of grade repetition. In suggesting how national assessment findings might be used to improve classroom teaching and learning, chapter 6 looks to the research literature—in particular to studies of school and teacher effectiveness—for guidance.

Caution is indicated in using the findings of research to support inferences drawn from national assessment data. Studies may not be technically adequate, or their findings may not be relevant to the context in which the national assessment was carried out. Potential problems will be magnified if the research was carried out in other countries. In particular, if those countries are economically developed, findings may not be relevant to a developing country. For example, the conclusion that small class sizes are associated with superior student achievement tends to be based on U.S. studies in which a class had 20 or fewer students (see, for example, Finn and Achilles 1990). Classes of this size are rare in developing countries.

DETERMINATION OF A SYSTEMWIDE OR TARGETED INTERVENTION

An important distinction in determining action is whether it will be systemwide or targeted on particular subpopulations or sectors of the education system. Systemwide action is intended to improve the performance of all students, and it includes improved instructional techniques, curriculum reform, and textbook reform. A teacher-training initiative could be systemwide or targeted. Other targeted interventions include a variety of provisions. First, an intervention may provide additional resources for students with special learning needs (for example, early prevention programs or remedial reading programs). Second, an intervention may involve various actions and policies, such as removing or alleviating pedagogical obstacles to performance (for example, lack of learning materials or poor-performing teachers) and economic barriers (for example, school fees or forgone labor). These actions may be designed to directly affect the performance of students in subgroups of the population, such as students from lower socioeconomic backgrounds, children displaced by civil unrest, orphans, linguistic minorities, students in small rural schools, or girls (in some societies). Third, an intervention may be designed to indirectly affect the cognitive performance of students (for example, parent involvement programs or nutritional and school meal programs) (see Willms 2006; World Bank 2004). Targeted interventions often require schools to develop and submit a plan that describes how they propose to use additional resources to improve student learning.

COMPLEXITY OF POLICY FORMATION AND DECISION MAKING

Chapter 1 noted that a range of political factors can play a role in determining the form of a national assessment. This chapter now addresses the complexity of policy and decision making following an assessment in the political environment outlined in chapter 1.

Policy making is not a simple linear process in which a problem is identified, possible solutions are considered, and implementation strategies are devised. Rather, it involves complex political activities, including negotiation, compromise, and responses to pressures and lobbies from a wide range of sources that must fit into preexisting belief patterns and value systems (see Blalock 1999). In reaching a decision, a policy maker may find the results of an assessment of value, but he or she will also need to take into account numerous political and other considerations on both national and local levels. Such considerations include politicians' views (ideological positions or concern about voter response and electability), budget availability, views and interests of stakeholders and interest groups, traditional views, and current fashions.

The relationship between a national assessment and political factors has positive aspects. For example, political forces can sometimes be harnessed to support the use of assessment findings. In particular, support for policy and decisions based on assessment findings will be enhanced if key stakeholders have been actively involved in the assessment from the early design stage. Certainly, at all stages, stakeholders should be kept in touch with relevant aspects of policy formation and decision making to ensure that they understand the need and rationale for reform. Representing stakeholders' interests on a steering committee that supervises the implementation of the national assessment can achieve this end (see Greaney and Kellaghan 2008, volume 1 in this series). Policy makers, in seeking to enlist support for reform, may also need to invoke principles widely accepted throughout the community, such as the provision of equal opportunities for all students, the importance of ensuring that the quality of student learning justifies the expenditure involved, and the need to provide a firm basis for the development of both individual students and the national economy.

The close connection between a national assessment and the political arena, although holding the prospect of improving policy formation and decision making, is not without its dangers. If an assessment becomes embroiled in political conflict, it is unlikely to play a major role in improving student learning. In Argentina, reflecting tensions between central and provincial authorities regarding their spheres of influence, information from assessments was used primarily to legitimate national policies and reforms and to regulate provincial authorities, rather than, for example, to design compensatory policies (Benveniste 2002; Gvirtz and Larripa 2004). A somewhat similar situation arose in the Arab Republic of Egypt, where local directorates of education refused to cooperate in a nationally designed assessment because they perceived it to reflect a hidden agenda to increase the control of central government (Carroll 1996).

The situation in Uruguay was different but also involved a conflict between powerful stakeholders. Fearful that the results of a national assessment would be used for teacher accountability, teachers' unions refused to cooperate until agreement was reached that reports on school performance would not be published, that the influence of student background on achievement would be given due recognition, and that teachers would not be held directly accountable for student performance (Benveniste 2002; Ravela 2005). This conflict was resolved through negotiation. Results were not used to hold teachers accountable, and Uruguay provides some of the more interesting examples of the use of national assessment findings to improve student learning (see chapter 6).

CONCLUSION

This chapter's description of the translation of findings into policy and action following a national assessment has identified two major issues. The first relates to the complexity of policy and decision making, the institutional capacity to absorb and use information, and the need to take account of a variety of vested interests in the process. The second major issue relates to the evidence used to interpret the findings of an assessment and to reach a conclusion about the most appropriate ways to proceed in designing policies or interventions that will address problems identified in the assessment with the objective of improving student learning.

One could argue that the basis for decision making would be strengthened if strategies to improve student learning suggested by national assessment findings were evaluated in an experimental or quasi-experimental study (see chapter 8). For several reasons, however, including time constraints, cost, and availability of personnel with the required technical skills, this course of action is unlikely. In most cases, policy and decision makers will, at best, rely on dissemination of findings to promote conceptualization and greater understanding of issues, discussion of findings by stakeholders, and consideration of relevant research, even though research may not have originated in the country in which the assessment was carried out.

CHAPTER 5

NATIONAL ASSESSMENT FINDINGS, POLICY, AND EDUCATIONAL MANAGEMENT

Policy makers, a category that includes politicians, educational administrators, and managers such as senior officials in a ministry of education, are the primary audience for national assessment results. Even when the results have implications for work by other stakeholders (for example, curriculum developers, teacher trainers, or classroom teachers), ministry officials will likely have a role to play in formulating policy, in issuing information or directives, or in providing resources. This chapter brings to the attention of policy and decision makers a range of potential and actual uses of findings in policy deliberations and educational management.

Four of the uses relate to providing information about the state of education and particularly about student achievement: (a) describing achievement, (b) describing resources, (c) monitoring achievement, and (d) reviewing the education system. A further five relate to the use of that information to address deficiencies identified in the assessment: (e) formulating general policy and assisting in decision making in conjunction with other information, (f) setting standards, (g) providing additional resources to schools (systemwide or targeted), (h) supporting curriculum revision, and (i) revising textbooks.

DESCRIBING ACHIEVEMENT

The basic purpose of a national assessment is to provide information on student achievement—particularly its shortcomings—which is a prerequisite for intervention (Aguerrondo 1992). Furthermore, the information is likely to be unique because it will not normally be available from other sources. Although education ministries routinely collect information about inputs to the education system (for example, student numbers, physical facilities, curriculum materials, teacher-student ratio), a national assessment provides information on the outcomes of the educational investment that inputs represent. Policy makers who have read a report of the findings of a national assessment, such as that outlined in chapter 2, will have an overall picture of student learning that, inevitably, even if not explicitly related to expectations, will invite judgment about the adequacy of student achievement. They are also likely to obtain information on specific domains of achievement with which students are experiencing difficulty, as well as data on the achievements of subgroups in the population.

A national assessment report usually presents information on achievement in the form of mean scores. Mean scores in themselves, however, provide only limited information for decision making. More meaningful descriptions of achievement, in the form of proficiency levels (what students know and can do), as described in chapter 2, provide a more informed basis for decisions and action.

Useful information can also be obtained when variance in achievement is partitioned into between- and within-school components (see chapter 2). Large between-school differences are sometimes interpreted as indicating disparity in learning opportunities in the education system. Policy makers should treat such an interpretation with caution, however, because it does not take into account differences between schools in factors over which the school may have little control (the characteristics of students when they enroll and the continuing effects of those characteristics on the work of the school).

Between-school differences in achievement may still merit the attention of policy makers because they may provide guidance on intervention. When between-school differences in a region are relatively low, and if financial resources are limited, intervention in some schools and not in others would probably not be justified. In contrast, targeting low-performing schools would be justified in regions with large between-school differences.

DESCRIBING RESOURCES

A national assessment frequently collects information on the resources available in schools. For example, India's national assessment in 2000 established that over 90 percent of schools had a school bell, a blackboard, chalk, and an eraser; close to three-quarters had safe drinking water; but less than 40 percent had separate toilets for girls (Singh and others n.d.).

Several national assessments in Africa provide evidence of lack of resources. In Kenya, for example, many schools had an inadequate number of desks and textbooks (Nzomo, Kariuki, and Guantai 2001). Furthermore, radio broadcast programs to schools did not reach a minimum of one-third of students, who did not have access to school radio (table 5.1). In Zanzibar, an assessment highlighted a serious shortage of classroom furniture (for example, desks and chalkboards) and supplies (for example, textbooks and pencils) (Nassor and Mohammed

TABLE 5.1

Percentages of Schools Possessing Selected Basic School Facilities: Kenya

Equipment	Percent	Standard error
Computer	1.2	0.77
Duplicator	19.9	3.11
Fax machine	0.5	0.35
Film projector	0.4	0.27
Overhead projector	0.3	0.30
Photocopier	1.1	0.70
Radio	66.4	4.31
Tape recorder	10.9	2.38
Television	3.2	1.74
Typewriter	27.5	3.70
Videocassette recorder	1.3	0.77

Source: Based on Nzomo, Kariuki, and Guantai 2001: table 3.1.4.

TABLE 5.2

Percentages of Schools Possessing School Facilities, 1990–2002: Malawi

Equipment	SACMEQ I	SACMEQ II
Chalk	95.2	96.4
Classroom library	13.3	20.4
Cupboard	17.8	51.2
One or more bookshelves	14.7	17.6
Teacher chair	42.3	50.5
Teacher table	40.7	47.7
Usable writing board	84.8	94.5
Wall chart	56.6	58.2

Source: Postlethwaite 2004b. Reproduced with permission, EFA Global Monitoring, UNESCO.
Note: The Southern and Eastern Africa Consortium for Monitoring Educational Quality (SACMEQ) is an international nonprofit developmental organization of 15 ministries of education in Southern and Eastern Africa that work together to share experiences and expertise in developing the capacities of education planners to apply scientific methods to monitor and evaluate the conditions of schooling and the quality of education. SACMEQ has completed two major education policy research projects (SACMEQ I and SACMEQ II).

1998). In Nigeria, few schools had maps (13 percent), charts or posters (15 percent), or sports equipment (5 percent). Teachers' responses to questionnaire items also pointed to the presence of high levels of concern over a lack of teaching materials, as well as low regard for teachers, poor conditions of service, and irregular payment of salaries (Nigeria Federal Ministry of Education 2000).

In Malawi, monitoring of changes in the provision of classroom resources between 1998 and 2002 revealed progress for all facilities (table 5.2). In Zimbabwe, a 1990 review showed schools in Matabeleland South had fewer resources than those in other regions of the country. A follow-up study in 1995 found no improvement (Postlethwaite 2004b).

MONITORING ACHIEVEMENT

If data are available from assessments carried out at different times, trends in achievement (whether it is improving, remaining the same, or deteriorating) can be identified (see chapter 2). This information has sometimes been used to monitor the effects on student achievement of changes in the education system (for example, change in language of instruction or increase in class size). In the United States, data from the national assessment (the National Assessment of Educational Progress, or NAEP) have been used to monitor the major reform initiative No Child Left Behind. In addition to the NAEP monitoring, each state is required to monitor the progress of all students in grades 3 through 8 on its own tests of reading, mathematics, and science. Many states reported significant improvement over the years; however, NAEP results did not reflect this improvement. The improvement recorded from 2003 to 2005, especially in grade 8, was much higher on state tests than on the NAEP test. In Maryland, for example, eighth-grade students who had a reported improvement of 12 percentage points in mathematics on the state test showed no improvement on the NAEP test (de Vise 2005). The difference seemed to occur because of the importance ascribed to the state tests, which had sanctions attached to them. Consequently, teachers focused their teaching on state test content, producing the subsequent increases in test scores without a concomitant improvement in the skills that the test was originally designed to measure (see Madaus and Kellaghan 1992).

In Uruguay, considerable improvement has been reported in the performance of sixth-grade students between 1996 and 2002 on the national assessment. Moreover, the improvement was especially marked among students in "very disadvantaged" schools, in which the percentage of students achieving an "acceptable" level on the test increased from 37.1 to 54.8. This increase is greater than the increase over the same period in schools in social contexts described as "very favorable," which was from 57.1 to 66.5 percent (Ravela 2006).

In some education systems, a national assessment in the same curriculum area and with the same population is carried out every year. If the aim is simply to monitor standards, this procedure would seem unnecessary, as well as very expensive. Most industrial countries that monitor achievement levels do so less frequently. In the United States, for example, where financial and technical resources are much less likely to be a problem than in developing countries, the NAEP in mathematics and reading is carried out every two years.

A perusal of the results of national assessments that have been running for several decades indicates that large changes in the achievements of students in an education system do not occur over a short time, even when efforts have been made to address problems identified in an assessment. Given this situation, a four- to five-year interval between assessments seems reasonable. Indeed, if national assessments administered over a short time span reported large changes, the equivalence of the tests and procedures used in the assessments would be open to question. Moreover, in many countries, the key source of change in performance over time will be changes in who is attending school. Rising participation rates create problems of comparability that require careful analysis. This and other problems in measuring change in performance over time can arise because of changes in curricula, language, and expectations, as well as from technical issues, such as when assumptions in measurement models (especially item response modeling) are not met or when student scores regress to the mean (Goldstein 1983).

REVIEWING THE EDUCATION SYSTEM

In many countries, the findings of a national (or regional) assessment have been mentioned in reviews of educational policy and provision or have been used to support major reform initiatives (see table 5.3).

The Dominican Republic provides a good example of the use of national assessment results in a major review of the education system, which was followed by a series of ambitious strategies to improve educational quality (box 5.1). The review provided the main input to meetings of regional teams of officials and members of communities and school networks that explored the reasons for poor performance and proposed strategies for addressing them.

FORMULATING GENERAL POLICY AND ASSISTING IN DECISION MAKING

Valid objective evidence on the condition of education, which a well-designed and well-implemented national assessment can provide, should serve to inject an objective component into decisions and help to ensure that cognizance is taken of empirical evidence as well as

TABLE 5.3

Selected Countries That Used National Assessment Results in Reviewing the Education System

Country	Examples of some claimed uses
Argentina	Instituted a program of school inspection
Bolivia	Linked assessment data to a program for child nutrition
Burkina Faso	Provided input for country analysis
Cuba	Strengthened preschool and early childhood care programs
Kenya	Led to benchmarks for providing facilities
Kuwait	Provided support for the policy of introducing classroom libraries
Malawi	Provided input for reform program
Mauritius	Used data to support national sector study
Namibia	Used by national commission
Nepal	Supported major government reform program
Niger	Provided input for country analysis
Sri Lanka	Provided input for national sector strategy for education
Uganda	Used to prepare educational reform program
Uruguay	Used to support a policy of expanding an equity program for full-time schools
Vietnam	Used to establish benchmarks for providing facilities (desks per pupil, books per pupil)
Zanzibar (Tanzania)	Used in review of educational policies, standards, and benchmarks
Zimbabwe	Used in commission review

Sources: Authors' compilation based on Arregui and McLauchlan 2005; Bernard and Michaelowa 2006; Ferrer 2006; Kuwait Ministry of Education 2008; Murimba 2005; Nzomo and Makuwa 2006; Ravela 2002.

personal biases, vested interests, anecdotal evidence, myths, and other forms of "accumulated wisdom" (see box 5.2). Furthermore, the concrete and persuasive evidence that an assessment can provide can help highlight problems in the education system related to access, quality, efficiency, or equity that might otherwise go unnoticed—or at any rate unattended. Nevertheless, the information derived from a national assessment will not identify ready-made policy or courses of action for the policy maker or other potential user. For one thing, as already noted, a national assessment provides just one piece of information to be considered in the context of a variety of other factors, including the

BOX 5.1

Using Assessment Results to Promote Reforms: Dominican Republic

In March 2005, Dominican Republic officials from each of the country's 17 national regions met to discuss their area's students' results in the most recent national tests for the end of the basic (8th grade) and secondary or *bachillerato* (12th grade) levels, as well as those obtained by students at the end of 4th grade. They looked at national averages in the various curricular subjects and themes or strands, as well as at the difference between their own and other regions' outcomes and of both of these with the national average. They looked at differences between private, public, and publicly funded/privately run schools. While no standards against which to compare performance were available, some definitions of what competencies or skills or what contents had been tested were offered to regional administrators and school principals.

This was one of the main inputs for a recently initiated process of system strategic planning, in which 17 regional and 101 district-level teams of officials and distinguished community members have jointly reviewed their main strengths and weaknesses for managing a change process focused on quality enhancement and are now drafting district and regional educational development plans with learning improvement as the main goal. Some districts have moved on in a very short time span to establish school networks, whose staff is meeting periodically to further analyze their region's national test results and to reflect on possible causes of unsatisfactory performance. While no strong evidence exists about the impact of various determining factors, some decisions have been taken rapidly at the district level on the basis of best available experience-based knowledge. One such example is the decision to share the few available qualified science teachers among several network schools. Another is the establishment of teacher networks to discuss challenges met in the course of efforts to improve learning comprehension capacities.

While it is too early to say whether these regional and district improvement plans based on assessment-generated information will have a lasting impact, it is clear to current authorities that the organization of these meetings has been far more mobilizing than the former strategy of sending reports to individual schools and students throughout the country.

Source: Arregui and McLauchlan 2005: 32–33. Reproduced with permission.

> **BOX 5.2**
>
> **Myths about Education in the United States**
>
> A national assessment can help discredit myths such as the following:
>
> 1. Reading achievement in the United States has declined in the past 25 years.
> 2. Forty percent of U.S. children cannot read at a basic level.
> 3. Twenty percent of U.S. children are dyslexic.
> 4. Children from the baby-boomer generation read better than do students today.
> 5. Students in the United States are among the worst readers in the world.
> 6. The number of good readers has been declining.
> 7. California's test scores declined dramatically because of whole-language instruction.
>
> *Source:* McQuillan 1998.

availability of resources (personnel and material) and the vested interests of stakeholders.

Considerable variation exists in national assessment reports in the extent to which they draw implications from assessment data and make recommendations for action or leave these activities to users. Some reports actually go well beyond what seems justified on the basis of the assessment findings in their recommendations (for example, in specifying the details of an intervention for students in rural schools or in suggesting approaches to the teaching of reading or mathematics). Such recommendations, if made, would need to be supported by other research evidence.

Policy makers and senior ministry of education officials may need assistance in interpreting the findings of a national assessment. A major aim of the Southern and Eastern Africa Consortium for Monitoring Educational Quality was, in fact, to promote capacity building by equipping educational planners in member countries with the technical ability to monitor and evaluate schooling and the quality of education. A particular feature of its approach was its "learning by doing" training for planners, whom it sought to involve directly in the conduct of studies (SACMEQ 2007). The World Bank Institute implemented a similar capacity-building program in Africa and South Asia.

Although a good deal of evidence indicates that national assessments have contributed to deliberations about educational policy and reform, independent objective evidence to indicate that assessment results actually affected policy is limited. An exception is found in Chile, where the results of its national assessment were instrumental in 1997 in convincing the National Congress, on learning that 40 percent of students did not understand what they read, that substantial changes in education were required (Schiefelbein and Schiefelbein 2000). Subsequently, national assessment findings played a role in several policy decisions, including the following (Meckes and Carrasco 2006):

- Directing technical and economic support from the national government to the most disadvantaged populations (as defined by learning outcomes) to provide a school feeding program and other assistance to poor students (a program that accounts for 5 percent of the overall public sector education budget)
- Defining the criteria for targeted interventions by the Ministry of Education
- Developing programs to improve educational quality and equity
- Defining incentives and goals for improvement
- Evaluating specific policies and programs
- Providing data for educational research purposes.

SETTING STANDARDS

In recent years, educational policy makers and curriculum authorities in many countries have increasingly emphasized setting standards and specifying what students should be able to do at the end of a number of stages of their formal schooling. National assessment results can assist in this task by operationalizing standards or achievement targets in key subject areas and by providing baseline indicators for monitoring progress over time. The Romanian government, for example, prompted in part by the poor findings of its grade 4 national assessment, used the results to provide baseline information for monitoring future achievement levels (Bethell and Mihail 2005). It also used the poor results of rural students as a justification for the development of its Rural Education Project supported by the World Bank.

Policy makers, donor agencies, and others should approach standard setting with some caution and, in particular, should set realistic targets for desired rates of improvement. In Peru, some policy makers suggested a 100 percent improvement in average scores in a nine-month period (Arregui and McLauchlan 2005). This goal is impossible to meet, especially if it is based on scale scores, which do not usually have zero points. The city of Bogotá in Colombia set a cutoff point for "acceptable" performance that less than 2 percent of schools were achieving at the time (Arregui and McLauchlan 2005). The U.S. No Child Left Behind target of 100 percent "proficiency" on state tests by 2014 seems to fall into the category of unrealistic targets. In 2003, no state or large district had anything close to 100 percent of students achieving at even the basic level, much less the proficient level, at either grade 4 or grade 8 in reading or mathematics (Linn 2005a).

Variation in defining terms such as *reading proficiency* and *mathematics proficiency* has given rise to problems in making inferences about what assessments say about the achievements of students. Evidence from the United States, for example, indicates that the meaning of *proficiency* in the NAEP differs from its meaning in state assessments. For example, in the neighboring states of Maryland and Virginia, the percentage of students rated proficient in reading and mathematics on NAEP tests differed from the percentage on state tests (de Vise 2005). The data in table 5.4 show that as many as 85 percent of Delaware

TABLE 5.4

Ranking of Grade 4 Students Rated at or above Proficient on State and National Assessments, 2005: United States

State	State (% proficient) (1)	NAEP (% proficient)[a] (2)	Difference (1) − (2)
Delaware	85	34 (1.2)	51
Idaho	87	33 (1.4)	54
North Carolina	83	29 (1.4)	54
Oregon	81	29 (1.5)	52
South Dakota	87	33 (1.3)	54

Source: Adapted from Stoneberg (2007), with permission.
a. Standard errors for NAEP are in parentheses.

students were deemed proficient on the state test, but as few as 34 percent on the NAEP test.

PROVIDING RESOURCES TO SCHOOLS

One possible reaction to the findings of a national assessment is to increase resources in schools. Provision could be at the system level, or it could be targeted to particular schools or populations.

System-level provision was a feature of action following a national assessment in a number of countries. In Kenya, where many schools were found to lack basic facilities (for example, desks and textbooks), the government decided to introduce benchmarks for classroom facilities, which implied a commitment to ensure that all schools would be provided with the facilities (Nzomo and Makuwa 2006). In Zimbabwe, special funds were provided for classroom supplies and management of school libraries, and training programs were initiated (Madamombe 1995). In the Dominican Republic, as indicated in box 5.1, scarce science teachers were reallocated among schools (Arregui and McLauchlan 2005).

Targeted intervention is implemented when the findings of an assessment reveal an association between a school's resources and student achievement. Thus, if the achievements of students in small rural schools were found to be lower than the national average, a decision might be made to grant additional resources to the schools. In Queensland, Australia, for example, schools with students who scored poorly (bottom 15 percent) in a literacy and numeracy assessment were allocated additional funds (Forster 2001). In Kuwait, findings that showed that students in classrooms with libraries or "reading corners" scored higher on a literacy test (the Progress in International Reading Literacy Study test) than did students in other classrooms were used as evidence to support the policy of the Ministry of Education to install classroom libraries (Kuwait Ministry of Education 2008).

Although a sample-based assessment will not provide data on all schools, it can provide information on categories of schools (for example, schools in different locations, schools of different types, schools serving populations of varying socioeconomic levels), thereby supplying a basis for targeted intervention for school categories. Intervention on this basis would seem defensible, though care obviously is required in identifying the schools that will benefit. In most systems, the focus would be on schools serving students who are likely to come from a disadvantaged background (for example, schools in which the level of parents' education is low). In some countries, school type or location can be a good indicator of who should benefit. National census data; educational management information system data; and information from school inspectors, supervisors, and advisers can also be helpful in identifying schools.

Although the national assessment system in Chile is census based, the provision made for low achievement could be relevant following a sample-based assessment if an adequate system of school identification is in place. Additional resources, including textbooks, classroom libraries, and pedagogical materials, were allocated to Chilean schools in areas with a high proportion of students from socially disadvantaged backgrounds who had performed poorly in the assessment (González, Mizala, and Romaguera 2002; Wolff 1998). After-school activities were also provided, school-community relations were developed, and schools were supervised between 8 and 16 times a year by provincial and central officials (Arregui and McLauchlan 2005).

When policy makers consider providing additional resources to schools following a national assessment, they must decide whether the allocation will be on a permanent or limited-time basis. A limited-time initiative may be considered preferable for a number of reasons. First, given that overall resources are limited, placing a time limitation on provision of resources to targeted schools might be more palatable to other schools and interests, which could see the additional resources as taking away from the resources that might have been available to them. Second, provision on a temporary basis is more likely to result in a more intensive intervention, which might include, for example, assistance in the use of resources. Third, international donor assistance has traditionally favored initiatives that are clearly defined and limited in time scale (Chapman and Snyder 2000).

SUPPORTING CURRICULUM REVISION

Curriculum revision is more frequently associated with international assessments than national assessments, probably because an international assessment can provide information on how students in an education system perform on an achievement test relative to students in other jurisdictions (the attained curriculum). The assessment may also provide comparative information derived from curriculum documents (the intended curriculum that operates at the education system level) and on the amount of time or emphasis accorded domains of achievement (the implemented curriculum that operates at the classroom level).

A national assessment can also provide information relevant to curriculum implementation or reform—most obviously, when students' actual achievements are compared to intended outcomes, as specified or implied in curriculum documents, and discrepancies are identified. Such a comparison can throw light on how the curriculum is being taught, what factors are associated with successful implementation, and whether curriculum expectations for student achievement are appropriate.

National and some state assessment findings have been associated with curriculum changes in a number of countries. In Brazil, the findings of the Paraná state assessment on student performance in major curriculum domains and the difficulties students exhibited were used to provide guidance to teachers on their instructional strategies (Ferrer 2006). In Thailand, the poor performance of students in areas of mathematics and science led to greater emphasis in curricula on teaching process skills and the application of knowledge (Pravalpruk 1996). In Guinea, national assessment results prompted the development of a national reading initiative to promote instruction in the early grades (R. Prouty, personal communication, Washington, D.C., May 15, 2005). Panama provides an example of a rather different use of assessment findings in the context of curriculum reform. In that country, one of the main purposes of the national assessment was to check on the impact of a new curriculum (Ferrer 2006).

A problem with most national assessments is that the adequacy of the intended curriculum is assumed, and assessment tasks are based on the curriculum. Analysis is then limited to how well students have acquired the knowledge and skills specified in the curriculum and, perhaps, how well the curriculum has been taught. However, making this assumption is to ignore the fact that in many developing countries the provision of education is oriented toward elites, with a resulting mismatch between the curriculum and the typical student (Glewwe and Kremer 2006).

In a number of countries, the appropriateness of the curriculum has been challenged in the wake of the findings of a national assessment. In a report in Bhutan, prepared following the 2003 grade 6 national assessment, curriculum overload was identified as a problem, and a strategic revision of the mathematics syllabus was recommended "to place less (or no) emphasis on algebra and geometry, or at least not at the level of sophistication currently expected of learners" (Bhutan Board of Examinations 2004: viii; see also Powdyel 2005). The views of stakeholders in interpreting assessment results can point to the need for curriculum reform. In Ethiopia, for example, feedback from teachers, students, and parents was used, in conjunction with an analysis of student performance on national assessment tests, to reach decisions about curriculum change (Z. Gebrekidan, personal communication, Addis Ababa, June 30, 2008).

The national assessment team in Uruguay, in consultation with teachers, went beyond what was officially described in curricula in their tests, which gave rise to debate about the validity and relevance of what was taught in schools. Over time, the conceptual framework of the test (together with student textbooks and teaching guides) became an alternative reference to the official national curriculum for teachers (Ferrer 2006).

The value of a national assessment for curriculum analysis and revision is likely to be enhanced if curriculum personnel are involved in identifying the precise skills to be assessed. They can, for example, help the test development process by clarifying the meaning of terms such as *reading*, which can be defined in a variety of ways, ranging from the ability to pronounce simple words, to the ability to read and comprehend simple sentences and paragraphs, to the ability to construct meaning from different forms of texts, including extended literary passages and informational texts (such as menus and timetables). Use of national assessment findings for curriculum revision will also be facilitated if curriculum personnel are involved in defining proficiency levels and in specifying the kind of data analysis that would facilitate their task (such as, in the case of numeracy, how well students perform on sets of items that assess simple computation with whole numbers or conceptual understanding of fractions and decimals). Finally, the national assessment team should draft a brief report on the implications of the findings of the assessment for curriculum reform and discuss it with the curriculum authority.

REVISING TEXTBOOKS

Ideally, textbooks should accurately reflect curriculum contents. A study carried out by the American Association for the Advancement of Science, however, found that the content of most popular middle and high school mathematics and science textbooks was not well aligned with a series of benchmarks contained in most state standards (Kulm, Roseman, and Treistman 1999), which are also used for setting assessment standards. The results of national (and international) assessments speak to this issue by identifying aspects of the curriculum that might merit more coverage or attention in new or revised editions of student textbooks and teacher manuals.

Little evidence indicates that national assessments have led directly to textbook revision, which usually occurs after substantial changes have been introduced to the official curriculum. A number of cases exist in Latin America, however, where changes in textbooks have proceeded in parallel with assessment activity. In Uruguay, for example, technical teams in charge of the national assessment and textbook revision worked from similar, though not identical, conceptual and pedagogical perspectives (P. Arregui, personal communication, Lima, September 22, 2008). In the area of language, new theories of instruction, which require exposure to a wider range of literary genres, were reflected in the content of national assessment tests and encouraged the production of a broad array of reading materials.

An interesting proposal regarding textbook provision followed a national assessment in Vietnam (World Bank 2004). In light of the finding that fewer than half of students had all the prescribed number of recommended textbooks and accompanying books, the national assessment team proposed that a shorter, more realistic set of books be identified by the curriculum authority, following which every effort should be made to ensure that every student received all the books.

Use of national assessment findings for textbook reform is likely to increase in the following contexts:

- If the assessment involves the active participation of the national curriculum authority in test development
- If the national assessment unit provides results to the curriculum authority in a form that is suitable for reviewing the quality of curriculum coverage in textbooks
- If the developers of standards or performance levels include individuals with expertise in curriculum development as well as educational measurement or assessment personnel.

CONCLUSION

The use that can be made of the findings of a national assessment depends in the first instance on the information that the assessment provides. Thus, those responsible for policy and management should specify their information needs at the planning stage of an assessment.

All national assessments provide a description of students' achievements. However, the uses that can be made of the information in deciding on intervention, for example, will depend to some extent on the detail in which achievement is described (for example, for separate domains or content areas of mathematics) and on the clues the assessment provides about the reasons for low achievement. Whether the data obtained in an assessment identify issues that might be addressed in curriculum or textbook revision will also be a function of the level of detail in achievement tests.

Not all national assessments collect information on resources. This information is likely to be sought if concern exists about provision throughout the system.

Assessment results can play a role in setting standards for student achievement in the education system. Of course, monitoring trends will be possible only if comparable data are available at different points in time.

In theory, assessment results can be used in formulating policy, in reviewing the education system, and in making decisions to provide additional resources to schools. The extent to which they are used for these purposes will, however, depend on a range of factors. These factors include the availability of reports of appropriate length in appropriate language geared to the interests and needs of policy makers and decision makers; the availability and use of adequate channels of communication; the availability of budgetary resources; and the interest, ability, and willingness of decision makers to absorb, interpret, and apply the findings of an assessment.

CHAPTER 6

NATIONAL ASSESSMENT FINDINGS AND TEACHING

Although the primary purpose of a national assessment may be to provide information to policy makers and education managers, student learning is unlikely to improve unless national assessment findings are used to develop policies and strategies directed toward changing school and classroom practices. Following an assessment, one approach is to introduce interventions in schools or categories of schools considered to be particularly in need of support (for example, providing additional physical resources or support for teachers to upgrade their knowledge or skills). In this situation, the central authority will clearly specify the terms of intervention. However, specific interventions do not normally follow a national assessment. More usually, results are published, leaving to key stakeholders, such as teachers, inspectors, advisers, and supervisors, the task of deciding on—and embarking on—changes in their practice that would be likely to influence student achievement. The issue this chapter addresses is how information obtained in a sample-based national assessment can be translated into effective practices to ameliorate deficiencies in individual schools and classrooms.

The chapter considers two approaches to this task. The first focuses on enhancing teachers' professional development by providing preservice and in-service courses. In the second, schools decide on the relevance of national assessment findings to their specific situation and, if the findings are considered relevant, devise strategies to deal with identified problems. The two approaches cannot always be readily distinguished. In-service courses (to upgrade teachers' knowledge and skills) may be school based, and some form of in-service training or workshops should ideally support the response of schools to a national assessment.

TEACHERS' PROFESSIONAL DEVELOPMENT

National assessment findings provide a rich source of data for ministries of education, regional bodies, and providers of preservice and in-service teacher education. This section first describes four sources of such data, which can be used to guide professional development activities for teachers. It then provides examples from a number of countries.

Sources of Data from a National Assessment to Guide Teachers' Professional Development

Four sources of data to guide professional development are available: (a) the framework of the assessment and sample questions, (b) students' performance on the assessment, (c) questionnaire responses, and (d) teachers' performance on an achievement test (about which some national assessments obtain information).

Framework of the national assessment and sample questions. The analysis of a curriculum area or construct contained in a national assessment framework, without any consideration of findings, can by itself be an important source of new perspectives and insights for teachers. For example, teachers attending in-service courses might be invited to review their practices in light of the analysis of mathematics achievement contained in the framework. They should ask, "Do I focus too much in my teaching on procedural knowledge (such as multiplication of numbers) at the expense of problem solving at higher cognitive levels, or do I pay insufficient attention to some aspects of the curriculum, such as teaching about shape and space?" In-service courses can also provide the opportunity for teachers to study sample questions, which are often released following a national assessment and might serve as models for their classroom assessment (Georgia Department of Education n.d.).

Students' performance on the assessment. Professional development courses might focus on aspects of the curriculum and of students' scholastic development that a national assessment finds problematic. A close examination of results can, for example, provide information on specific areas of reading (for example, detecting the unstated meaning in a text) or mathematics (for example, problem solving) where students—and by inference teachers—need support (see chapter 2).

Questionnaire responses. A national assessment provides information that can be used to design a course that is not limited to information obtained in tests about student achievement. Information obtained in questionnaires is also relevant. It can throw light on a range of factors relevant to teaching: social and economic conditions in which schools operate; problems that teachers encounter in teaching; teachers' appraisal of the availability, quality, and usefulness of resources (including student textbooks and teacher manuals); parents' and students' attitudes toward education; and students' motivation to learn (see Griffith and Medrich 1992). In the U.S. national assessment, information obtained from students and teachers in questionnaires, which subsequent analyses revealed to be important correlates of student achievement, prompted reflection by teachers. The information in the student questionnaire related to parents' level of education and educational resources in the home; the teacher questionnaire contained detailed information on how teachers taught mathematics (for example, how they addressed unique and routine problems, used textbooks and worksheets, had students solve real-world problems, and had students work with partners) (see Wenglinksy 2002).

An example from the 2003 Trends in International Mathematics and Science Study (TIMSS) shows how a question on the readiness of teachers to teach different aspects of the mathematics curriculum helped identify deficiencies in teacher knowledge that in-service training could address. In a report of the study, data were presented on the percentage of students whose teachers felt they were competent to teach specific topics (Mullis and others 2004). Table 6.1 presents an

TABLE 6.1
Percentages of Students Whose Teachers Reported They Were Ready to Teach Mathematics, TIMSS Data, Grade 8

	Percentage of students whose teachers report feeling they are ready to teach mathematics topics					
	Number			Algebra		
Selected countries	Representing decimals and fractions, using words, numbers, and number lines	Integers, including words, numbers, number lines, ordering integers, and operations (+, −, ×, and ÷) with integers	Numeric algebraic and geometric patterns of sequences	Simple linear equations and inequalities, and simultaneous (two variable) equations	Equivalent representations of functions as ordered pairs, tables, graphs, words, or equations	Attributes of a graph, such as intercepts on axes, and intervals
Bulgaria	100	100	99	100	100	100
Iran, Islamic Rep. of	98	98	90	98	94	87
Lebanon	98	100	93	96	95	95
Saudi Arabia	96	100	86	95	94	80
Serbia	91	90	93	90	90	90
Tunisia	99	98	87	71	74	71

Source: Extracted from Mullis and others 2004: 256.

excerpt from the report for two of five content areas in mathematics (number and algebra). The data suggest that in-service courses (as well as preservice courses) in most of the countries would do well to focus attention on teaching specific skills, such as the attributes of a graph. Similar questions could be included in a national assessment to help identify areas in need of attention in teacher education courses.

A teacher questionnaire can also provide information about teachers' experience with in-service courses and the needs that they believe in-service training could meet. In India and Bhutan, questionnaire data established that many teachers had little or no experience with in-service courses (Bhutan Board of Examinations 2004; Powdyel 2005; Singh and others n.d.). The need for courses in how to teach writing was revealed in Lesotho (M. C. Ramokoena, personal communication, Maseru, April 6, 2009).

Although this kind of information can provide guidance for teacher in-service programs, considerable skill is required to obtain it in a questionnaire. For example, problems such as those encountered in the Scottish national assessment (Assessment of Achievement Programme), in which data obtained from questionnaires were not sufficiently specific to establish associations between student achievement and school practices, need to be avoided (Robertson 2005).

Teachers' performance on an achievement test. Although courses designed to improve teachers' pedagogical skills are more common than ones that target their knowledge of subject matter, the need to address the latter may be more pressing than is generally recognized. The few national assessments that obtained information on teachers' knowledge of subject matter identified serious deficiencies. Following the grade 5 national assessment in Vietnam, in which the same test items were administered to teachers and students, the distribution of reading comprehension scores for students (the flatter distribution in figure 6.1) and for teachers (the steeper distribution on the right) could be displayed. The data show that the top 12 percent of students outperformed the bottom 30 percent of teachers.

In Pakistan's National Education Assessment System, the items administered to grade 4 students were also administered to teachers. As in Vietnam, the distributions of scores overlapped. Approximately

FIGURE 6.1

Reading Score Distributions of Pupils and Teachers: Vietnam

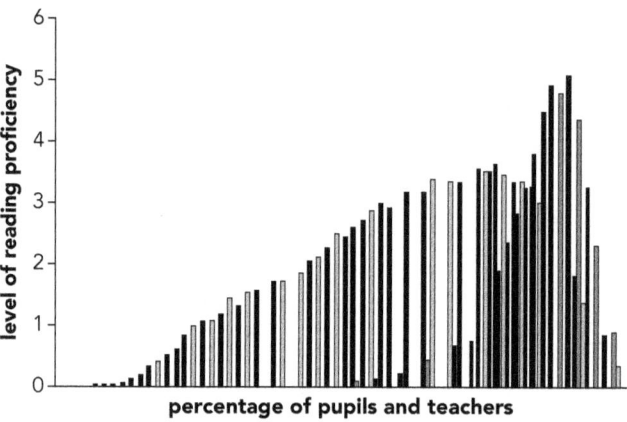

Source: World Bank 2004, vol. 1: figure 2.
Note: Pupils' reading scores are the flatter curve and teachers' scores the steeper curve.

BOX 6.1

Place-Value Matching Item: Pakistan

Which of these is the same as 4256?

A) Four thousand two hundred and fifty-six

B) Four thousand five hundred and twenty-six

C) Four thousand two hundred and fifty

D) Four hundred twenty-five thousand and six

Source: A. Tayyab, personal communication, Oxford, U.K., July 24, 2008.

3 percent of teachers scored below the mean score of students. Very few items were answered correctly by 90 percent of teachers (A. Tayyab, personal communication, Oxford, U.K., July 24, 2008). A closer look at the teacher data reveals that teachers performed poorly on items that assessed geometry, place value, and measurement. For example, only 42 percent correctly answered an item similar to the one presented in box 6.1, which required matching a four-digit number with its equivalent in words.

National assessments in Africa have demonstrated similar findings (Duthilleul and Allen 2005). Table 6.2 documents the percentage of teachers in a national assessment in Mozambique that were placed at eight levels of proficiency on a mathematics test designed for sixth-grade students. The description of the proficiency levels identifies the skills and knowledge that teachers at each level had acquired and, by implication, the skills and knowledge that they lacked. For example, all teachers achieved proficiency levels 1 and 2, but close to one in four teachers did not respond correctly to problem-solving items (levels 7 and 8).

TABLE 6.2

Percentage of Teachers Scoring at Each Mathematics Proficiency Level: Mozambique

Level	Description	Percent
Level 1: Prenumeracy	• Applies single-step addition or subtraction operations. Recognizes simple shapes. • Matches numbers and pictures. • Counts in whole numbers.	0.0
Level 2: Emergent numeracy	• Applies a two-step addition or subtraction operation involving carrying, checking (through very basic estimation), or conversion of pictures to numbers. • Estimates the length of familiar objectives. • Recognizes common two-dimensional shapes.	0.0
Level 3: Basic numeracy	• Translates verbal information presented in a sentence, simple graph, or table using one arithmetic operation in several repeated steps. • Translates graphical information into fractions. • Interprets place value of whole numbers up to thousands. • Interprets simple, common, everyday units of measurement.	0.3
Level 4: Beginning numeracy	• Translates verbal or graphic information into simple arithmetic problems. • Uses multiple different arithmetic operations (in the correct order) on whole numbers, fractions, and decimals.	2.9

(continued)

TABLE 6.2

Level	Description	Percent
Level 5: Competent numeracy	• Translates verbal, graphic, or tabular information into an arithmetic form to solve a given problem. • Solves multiple-operation problems (using the correct order of arithmetic operations) involving everyday units of measurement and whole and mixed numbers. • Converts basic measurement units from one level of measurement to another (for example, meters to centimeters).	4.6
Level 6: Mathematically skilled	• Solves multiple-operation problems (using the correct order of arithmetic operations) involving fractions, ratios, and decimals. • Translates verbal and graphic representation information into symbolic, algebraic, and equation form to solve a given mathematical problem. • Checks and estimates answers using external knowledge (not provided within the problem).	16.3
Level 7: Concrete problem solving	• Extracts and converts (for example, with respect to measurement units) information from tables, charts, and visual and symbolic presentations to identify and then solve multistep problems.	44.3
Level 8: Abstract problem solving	• Identifies the nature of an unstated mathematical problem embedded within verbal or graphic information, and then translates it into symbolic, algebraic, or equation form to solve the problem.	31.7

Source: Bonnet 2007. Reproduced with permission.

Other data from Vietnam (figure 6.2) show the extent to which teacher subject-matter knowledge and student performance in mathematics are related. As teachers' mean achievement score (based on the mean for a province) increases, the mean for students (also based on the mean for the province) rises (World Bank 2004). The findings prompted a recommendation that teachers with poor subject mastery be encouraged to participate in in-service courses to improve their knowledge as a means of decreasing the number of low-achieving students.

FIGURE 6.2

Grade 5 National Assessment in Mathematics in Vietnam: Correlation between Teacher and Pupil Provincial Mean Scores

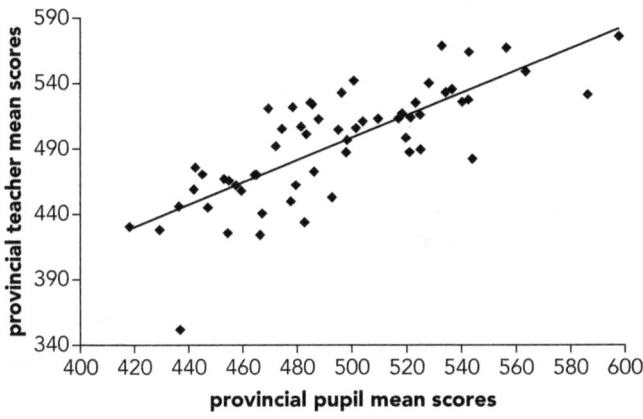

Source: World Bank 2004, vol. 1: figure 5.

Examples of Activities to Enhance Teacher Professional Development Following a National Assessment

There is relatively little evidence that policy makers or educational planners have used national assessment findings to determine the topics to be addressed in teacher education programs, except in some Latin American countries (Argentina, Brazil, Chile, Cuba, the Dominican Republic, Ecuador, Guatemala, Honduras, Uruguay, and the República Bolivariana de Venezuela) (Ferrer 2006). Some countries have used results as a basis for mass teacher-training events on national television (Cuba) and in reviews of the national assessment by educators, including teacher trainers (Dominican Republic). The Brazilian state of Minas Gerais provides a good example of the use of assessment data to improve teacher education (box 6.2). However, little information is available about the effect of these efforts on teacher competence (Arregui and McLauchlan 2005).

In Uruguay, where schools are the main audience for test results, the principal focus following an assessment is on investment in improving teachers' knowledge and ability to teach, with a particular emphasis on teaching reading and mathematics in schools serving students from

> **BOX 6.2**
>
> **Use of National Assessment Findings to Improve Teacher Education: Minas Gerais, Brazil**
>
> The Brazilian state of Mina Gerais took the following steps in the design and use of national assessment findings to improve teacher education:
>
> - The assessment set out to provide useful information to teacher-training institutions.
> - Formal collaboration took place among the 29 higher educational institutions in designing and administering tests, processing results, and delivering them to schools.
> - One university led the effort, with the support of the others.
> - The data were examined to identify students' reading problems revealed by the assessment.
> - Students attending preservice education courses were expected to study the assessment results to become familiar with education issues.
> - The results were used to develop teacher-training programs.
>
> *Source:* Ferrer 2006.

disadvantaged backgrounds. The approach seems to have had very positive results, reflected in an improvement over time in students' performance in assessments (see chapter 5). Significant features of the approach include the following (Ravela 2006):

- Item and error analysis of student performance
- Absence of high-stakes accountability
- Feedback to schools based on test results
- Professional development meetings for teachers to exchange ideas
- Targeting of schools on the basis of poverty, not achievement.

The large-scale in-service program attracted about 3,000 teachers from 300 to 500 poor urban schools each year (box 6.3). It featured some of the attributes of professional development programs generally found to lead to improvement in teachers' knowledge and skills, including a focus on content knowledge, ample opportunities for active learning, coherence with other activities, collective participation of teachers from the same school, and sufficient program time to have an impact (see Garet and others 2001).

> **BOX 6.3**
>
> **Main Features of a Teacher In-Service Program Based on National Assessment Results: Uruguay**
>
> In Uruguay, a large-scale in-service program had the following features:
>
> - Courses were held on Saturdays.
> - Teachers were paid for participation (around 25 percent of teachers' initial salary).
> - Participation was voluntary.
> - Participation was school based—teachers were admitted to the training program only if at least half the teachers (including the principal) in a school agreed to participate.
> - Sessions included groups of about 60 teachers. Teams from 5 to 10 schools joined together, providing an opportunity to share experiences both within and between schools.
> - Programs focused on schools in disadvantaged contexts, but students' achievements were not taken into account so that teachers from both well-performing and poorly performing schools could share experiences.
> - A group of supervisors and professors from teacher-training institutions, selected and trained for the program, conducted sessions.
> - The program focused on teaching approaches to mathematics, language, and natural and social sciences.
>
> *Source:* Ravela 2005.

Communication and political problems can inhibit efforts to influence teacher training, as was the case in Argentina, where a lack of communication was reported between the agencies responsible for teacher training and assessment (Ferrer 2006). Problems in Chile were attributed to the fact that teacher-training institutions were often ideologically opposed to the national assessment (Sistema de Medición de la Calidad de la Educación, or SIMCE) (Meckes and Carrasco 2006).

In-service courses and programs are frequently provided for head teachers in recognition of the vital role they play in the life of the school. In Uruguay, for example, in addition to workshops for teachers and supervisors, workshops were organized following a national assessment specifically to address the issues of head teachers (Benveniste 2002). In-service training for head teachers could be expected to cover a wide range of topics designed to provide knowledge and develop skills likely to contribute to the creation of an environment supportive of student learning. Questionnaires administered in a national assessment can help inform the content of this kind of in-service training, prompting educational authorities to organize courses to address one or more of the following (Murphy, Yff, and Shipman 2000):

- Skills of head teachers in managing school resources to provide a safe, efficient, and effective learning environment
- Their leadership skills to sustain a school culture and an instructional program that support student learning
- Their ability to assist teachers in developing teachers' knowledge and skills
- Their ability to analyze and address problems of discipline, school attendance, and staff morale
- Their ability to develop strategies to collaborate with families and communities in the work of the school (particularly if the community holds negative perceptions of the school)
- Their ability to understand, respond to, and influence the larger political, social, economic, legal, and cultural context.

FOCUS ON SCHOOLS AND CLASSROOM TEACHING

Ensuring that national assessment findings influence the practice of classroom teachers to improve student learning is a challenging and complex task. Little is known regarding the most effective strategies to use, which are likely to vary from one education system to another and from school to school.

This section addresses the situation in which the findings of a national assessment are disseminated and individual schools are left to interpret the findings' relevance and develop strategies to address problems that may be identified. Three specific procedural steps are described that seem essential if national assessment findings are to be used effectively: (a) communication of findings to teachers, (b) interpretation of findings by teachers and assessment of their relevance to their school, and (c) application of findings in strategies designed to improve student learning. Following a consideration of these steps, decisions that need to be made in planning an intervention are identified.

Communication of Findings

A variety of approaches is possible following a sample-based national assessment to inform teachers throughout the education system of findings: printed material and reports; seminars and workshops; and visits from inspectors, supervisors, and advisers. In some countries, teachers have access to national assessment reports on the Web.

A report can contain comments of a general nature and broad exhortation, or it can contain detailed information based on analysis of student performance. Uganda, where the results of its national assessment were limited to general messages sent in poster form to teachers in all schools for classroom display, provides an example of the former (box 6.4). Other countries provide more detailed

---

BOX 6.4

Poster Extract Published after National Assessment: Uganda

In Uganda, a poster with the following text was distributed to teachers for display in their classrooms:

We can do the following:

- Listen to instructions in English and respond appropriately
- Read a short piece of writing in English
- Carry out addition, subtraction, and multiplication of numbers
- Write some English words and sentences

Help us to learn to:

- Develop a wider vocabulary
- Read fast and fluently
- Write clearly and neatly
- Carry out division of numbers correctly
- Use knowledge already learnt in new situations in everyday life

Source: Uganda National Examinations Board n.d.

reports—primarily for teachers—that describe the achievements of students in terms of the curriculum areas that have shown particular strengths and weaknesses. Including practical suggestions that schools and teachers could use to improve student achievement will clearly augment the value of these reports.

A report to teachers in British Columbia, Canada, provides an example of a detailed description of student performance on an assessment. The report contained a series of tables indicating the percentage of students at the district level who answered each item in a test correctly, as well as the percentage of students who selected incorrect alternatives. It also provided an interpretation of what students were typically doing when choosing incorrect responses. Table 6.3 presents an example for a test of mathematics (patterns and relations).

In a similar vein, box 6.5 provides an example of an item that could be used in a group discussion to help teachers identify the common errors of students when they are presented with a basic mathematics computation item involving more than one step and a squared number.

TABLE 6.3

Percentage of Students Answering Items Correctly in a Mathematics Assessment: British Columbia, Canada

Item number	Percentage correct	Description of item	Comments on incorrect responses
2	53	A word problem involving division and finding of a remainder (dividing a number of objects into sets of a given size and finding how many are left over)	More than one-quarter (28%) subtracted rather than divided; 13% divided correctly but found an incorrect remainder.
21	55	A word problem involving multiplication, subtraction, and division (finding the greatest number of an item that can be purchased with change from an earlier purchase)	Common errors were calculating incorrectly (19%), ignoring part of the information (10%), and using only part of the information in the calculations (10%).

Source: Extracted from British Columbia Ministry of Education 1999.

> **BOX 6.5**
>
> **Mathematics Item**
>
> $5^2 - 3(4 - 1) =$
>
> A) −4   (13%)
> B) 10   (22%)
> C) 14   (27%)
> D) 16   (38%)
>
> *Source:* Authors' compilation.

The numbers in parentheses after each option represent the percentage of students who selected the option. Teacher discussion should lead to the following conclusions:

- A majority of students responded incorrectly and had not selected option D.
- Those who selected option A may not have known the significance of the index 2.
- Those who selected option B may have changed the sign inside the bracket because of the minus sign outside the bracket.
- Those who selected option C may have multiplied the 3 by 4 and then subtracted 1, instead of first subtracting 1 from 4.

Although reports to schools provide potentially valuable information for teachers, merely distributing materials to schools is unlikely to be effective for the following reasons:

- Teachers, bombarded by a variety of curriculum documents, may not see national assessment reports as a priority for their attention. A survey in a New Zealand city found that teachers were largely unaware of national assessment reports or of their potential for enhancing the quality of teachers' work. Although copies of reports had arrived in schools, very few teachers either knew of their existence or had read them (Lovett 1999).

- Reports, even when prepared specifically for schools and teachers, may not be sufficiently user-friendly (Arregui and McLauchlan 2005; OECD 2004).
- Teachers may need assistance in developing an understanding of a proposed reform and its relevance to the conditions in which they teach.
- Teachers will probably need assistance if they are to change their teaching to achieve objectives suggested in a reform (for example, to shift their focus from memorization and group recitation to procedures that will develop greater student engagement and more active involvement in learning) (Chapman and Snyder 2000; Grant, Peterson, and Shojgreen-Downer 1996; Ravela 2005; Snyder and others 1997).

Interpretation of Findings and Assessment of Their Relevance

Even without a national assessment, schools—especially if they serve students from an economically disadvantaged background—will usually be aware if a substantial number of their students are experiencing difficulty. In this situation, national assessment findings may be no more than a spur to reflection and action. Assessment findings, however, as well as reinforcing teachers' perceptions (if, for example, particular categories of school are identified as problematic), can provide indications of the nature of students' difficulties and clues to the factors that inhibit or foster student learning. Nevertheless, schools clearly need to take cognizance of the actual conditions in which they operate, which can vary considerably from one location to another.

In this regard, a variety of factors merit consideration. Schools differ in students' levels of achievement and in the causes of low achievement. Teachers differ in how well they know the content they are expected to teach and in their pedagogical skills and attitudes. Schools differ in the resources that are available, in the ways they use those resources, in the constraints under which they operate (such as very large classes), and in their capacity to change. They also differ in the social and economic circumstances in which they operate, in the readiness of their students for learning on arriving at school, and in the support they receive from homes and communities. Teachers need to reflect on these matters, gauging the relevance of the assessment findings to their situation. In particular, they need to determine the knowledge or skills that represent the greatest instructional needs and the kind of change that would be likely to be most effective.

Because a sample-based assessment does not provide information on standards of achievement in individual schools, schools need some way of determining how the achievements of their students compare with those of students in other schools if the national assessment findings are to be relevant. Uruguay addressed this issue by making the assessment instrument available to schools that did not participate in the national assessment. Although this approach allows all schools to compare the achievement of their students with national norms, it has the disadvantage that the ability to monitor achievement in the education system over time is compromised because widely available items presumably cannot be reused. An alternative approach would be to develop and make available to all schools a set of standardized tests of achievement that teachers could administer to their own students to determine their standing relative to national norms that the tests would provide. The value of the standardized tests would be greatly enhanced if they also provided diagnostic information about student achievements, which could provide a basis for remedial action.

Application of Findings

When the relevance of national assessment findings to a particular school is established, the school should review in detail the achievements of its students (identifying gaps and weaknesses in learning) and the circumstances that may be contributing to the situation. It should then devise strategies to address identified problems. Many teachers will find this task very difficult and will require considerable support. Support may take the form of guidelines and examples of good practice from the ministry of education, workshops for head teachers and subject specialists, or on-site support from inspectors or supervisors. All of these can contribute to deliberations at staff meetings.

Teachers may need specific help in (a) identifying aspects of their practice that need to change, (b) describing desired practices, (c) describing differences between existing and desired practices, and

(d) specifying stages in practices that will indicate movement toward desired practices. Moving through the stages will be an incremental process in which, it may be hoped, teachers will adapt existing practices in moving toward ones that are more likely to have a positive effect on student learning.

Some national assessment reports include specific recommendations for action (see box 6.6). The recommendations are specific to a particular country and curriculum and may not be relevant in other

---

BOX 6.6

Recommendations Following a National Assessment in Mathematics, Grade 5: Ireland

The following recommendations are from a guide that was published by the Irish Department of Education and Science in response to a national assessment:

- Teachers should support pupils' development in the "Shape & Space" content strand by engaging them in tasks involving reasoning about shape and space.

- Teachers should extend work relating to data collection, data analysis, and construction and interpretation of graphs to subjects such as geography and science. Opportunities should be sought to apply knowledge about the "Number," "Measures," and "Shape & Space" strands in other subject areas and in real-life contexts.

- Teachers should accord greater emphasis to the "Measures" strand by providing opportunities for pupils to transfer the knowledge and skills acquired in practical activities to nonroutine problems.

- Teachers should place greater emphasis on teaching higher-order mathematics skills, including "Applying" and "Problem Solving."

- Schools and teachers should support parents in developing their child's proficiency in mathematics by providing information on changes in curriculum and teaching methods, advice on engaging children in mathematics-related activities at home, and guidance on using homework (including the amount of time to allocate to homework) to support learning.

- Schools and teachers should extend the use of calculators and information and communication technologies to teach mathematics. Calculators and information and communication technologies should be used not only to develop skills such as basic computation, but also to enhance mathematical reasoning and problem-solving skills.

Source: Adapted from Surgenor and others 2006; also available at http://www.erc.ie.

settings. The point, however, is that when a national assessment includes recommendations, it can serve as a prompt or checklist to guide a series of staff discussions as the head teacher and teachers review the practice in their school and how it conforms with—or diverges from—the practice recommended in the national assessment report.

Very often, a national assessment report will not provide specific recommendations. In this case, teachers will have to rely more on their own resources in devising strategies to address areas of weakness in students' achievements identified in the assessment. In Uganda, following a consideration of assessment findings (for example, low performance in reading continuous text, in writing, and in geometry), a group of head teachers from a number of schools identified specific ways in which they felt they could improve the learning environment in their schools. These methods included improving the pacing of instruction in response to students' progress (or lack of it), checking teachers' schemes of work and lesson plans, involving students in making learning materials, and holding competitions among students in reading and numeracy tasks (Acana 2008).

A consideration of the findings of educational research can inform teachers' discussions at staff meetings and in other forums of ways to address problems identified in a national assessment. Because teachers are not likely to be familiar with research findings, the following pages summarize major findings that could inform their deliberations. Areas relevant to such deliberations are (a) research on school effectiveness (box 6.7), (b) research on teacher effectiveness (box 6.8), and (c) research on relationships between student learning and individual student and family factors (box 6.9).

Teachers should keep a number of factors in mind when considering the research. First, the findings are based for the most part on the results of studies carried out in industrial countries. The smaller number of studies in developing countries replicates those results in many respects, with the exception that a stronger association of student achievement with teacher quality and with the availability of resources (for example, textbooks) has been found (Reynolds 2000). Second, teachers may be more effective in some curriculum areas than in others. For example, the skills required for teaching art or laboratory science may differ from those required to teach language and mathematics (the curriculum areas investigated in most studies of school effectiveness). Third,

BOX 6.7

Discussion Topics: National Assessment Results and School Effectiveness Variables

Schools should consider in their discussions the following factors, which have been found in research to be related to school effectiveness:

- Orderly school environment
- High quality of head teacher's instructional leadership
- Positive school "culture" or "climate" (unity of purpose, with a focus on student learning)
- High expectations for student achievement and behavior
- Strong disciplinary environment
- High staff morale
- Opportunities for staff development
- Parental involvement
- Coordination and consistency of instruction across grade levels.

Sources: Lockheed and Verspoor 1991; Reynolds and Teddlie 2000.

BOX 6.8

Discussion Topics: National Assessment Results and Teacher Effectiveness Variables

Schools should consider in their discussions the following factors, which have been found in research to be related to teacher effectiveness:

- Knowledge of subject matter
- Management and organization of classrooms (for example, to ensure minimal disruption)
- Instructional practices (clarity of academic focus, pacing instruction to students' level, opportunities for students to practice and apply what they have learned, adequate curriculum coverage, and opportunities for students to learn)
- Ability to teach higher-order thinking skills
- Individualization of instruction

(continued)

BOX 6.8

- Collaborative learning that facilitates group work by students
- High expectations for achievement and behavior communicated to students
- Availability and adequacy of resources (textbooks and other instructional materials)
- Monitoring and assessment of student progress (use and frequency of precise reinforcement; appropriate questions that are at a suitable level of difficulty and require students to reflect, organize, and apply knowledge rather than simply recall information)
- Frequency and monitoring of homework
- Attendance
- Time spent on preparation for class
- Beliefs, perceptions, and assumptions (including expectations for student achievement).

Sources: Brophy and Good 1986; Fuller 1987; Teddlie and Reynolds 2000; Wang, Haertel, and Walberg 1993; Wenglinsky 2002.

BOX 6.9

Discussion Topics: National Assessment Results and Individual Student and Family Factors Associated with Student Learning

Research indicates that characteristics such as the following have significant effects on student achievement:

- Student characteristics (motivation, engagement in learning, nutritional status, and illnesses)
- Attendance
- Parents' educational or income level
- Family support (having high expectations for scholastic achievement, being involved in schoolwork, assisting with homework, reading to children or having children read to family members, and liaising with child's teacher)
- Demands on student outside school (work or child-minding responsibilities).

Source: Authors' compilation.

teachers may be more effective with some categories of students than others (Campbell and others 2004).

School effectiveness. Factors generally associated with effectiveness at the level of the school (box 6.7) underline the importance of the head teacher's role, as well as the importance of developing a school culture that emphasizes student learning. Supporting conditions, such as school discipline and morale, also figure in these factors. Staff discussions should focus on the link between the national assessment findings and the school effectiveness factors that are most relevant to the school's situation.

Teacher effectiveness. Empirical evidence available for over a century on the key role that the home background of students plays in their ability to learn may at times have led commentators to underestimate the effects of school characteristics and, in particular, of teachers' classroom practices. Recent research based on data collected for the U.S. National Assessment of Educational Progress, using sophisticated statistical analysis, challenges this view. The findings of the research indicate that classroom practices (for example, a focus on teaching higher-order thinking skills, the application of problem-solving techniques to unique problems, and the individualization of instruction) affected students' mathematics achievement in eighth grade at least as strongly as student background (Wenglinsky 2002).

The factors found to be associated with the effectiveness of teachers in their classrooms (box 6.8) identify teachers' subject-matter knowledge and pedagogical skills. Instructional conditions that are particularly important include opportunity to learn, time on task, structured teaching, assessment and feedback to students, availability of adequate resources, and use of multiple paths to the solution of problems to accommodate the variation that one finds in any classroom in students' knowledge and experience (Scheerens 1998; Wenglinsky 2002). Specification of high expectations for student achievement in the classroom reinforces the need for high expectations at the school level (box 6.7). The relationship between school effectiveness and teacher effectiveness also finds expression in the need to coordinate instruction across grade levels. Therefore, school staff discussions of a national assessment should consider the implications of the findings for teaching at all grades and, in particular, at grades below the one at which the assessment was carried out.

Ideally, the mechanism to achieve changes in teachers' practices will involve reviews by the school's staff to examine and interpret student performance data and to develop teaching strategies designed to raise student achievement. Support from inspectors, supervisors, or advisers will be important as teachers strive to apply what they have learned in their classrooms. Change in the classroom is more likely to occur and to be sustained when the following specific conditions are met (Elmore and Burney 1999; Fullan 2001; Reezigt and Creemers 2005):

- The nature of problems (for example, poor performance in division of decimals) and their possible causes are clarified.
- Improvement needs are identified, and specific goals are set (relating, for example, to achievement in particular domains, attitudes, students' role in the learning process, attendance).
- A plan (with specific steps) with priority areas for instruction is developed to address identified deficiencies.
- Expectations are set for student achievement.
- Strategies are developed on the basis of discrepancies identified between present and desired practice.
- Student progress is monitored on a regular basis.
- The focus is on the concrete application of general ideas.
- Teachers are exposed to actual desired practice rather than to descriptions of practice.
- Opportunities are provided for teachers to interact with each other and with inspectors or supervisors in a collaborative work culture.
- Progress in implementing the plan is evaluated and reflected on (for example, to determine if goals have been achieved).

The less tangible aspects of some of the items specified for teacher effectiveness in box 6.8 should be noted. If, as has been stated, belief systems underlying the value and purpose of a curriculum and teachers' expectations and aspirations for their students are more important than changing details of a curriculum or teaching strategies (Anderson 2002; Robertson 2005), then strategies to improve student learning will need to respond to a wider range of circumstances than has normally been the practice.

Student, family, and community factors. In their discussions of national assessment findings, head teachers and teachers should consider research on individual student, family, and community factors that affect student learning (see box 6.9). If problems related to these factors are identified, procedures designed to have an indirect impact on students' cognitive development may be indicated in areas other than at the school or classroom level. Options at the individual student level could include providing school meals or supplements for nutritional deficiencies. However, such provision would normally require a decision at a higher level or the involvement of parents because an individual school is unlikely to be able to meet the costs involved. A school would not be able to do much about parents' formal educational levels either, but it could advise parents on the characteristics of a family environment that support children's learning. For example, findings of the Vietnam national assessment (see chapter 2) prompted the recommendation that parents be advised about the usefulness of providing a private space at home for students to study, as well as the need to minimize their children's absence from school (World Bank 2004).

In their review of national assessment findings, school personnel might well reflect on ways to strengthen the link between school and students' home lives. Schools in many countries have formal links with families, though in some cases they exist in name only. Links may need to be reinvigorated and developed to play an active role in increasing the involvement of families in activities that encourage and promote student learning. A wide range of strategies is available for this purpose. Such strategies include (a) involving parents in governance and advocacy on behalf of the school (for example, in a parent-teacher association or a school management board); (b) having parents assist with noninstructional activities in the school; (c) holding workshops and lectures to discuss school policies or home conditions that promote learning; and (d) using programs to involve parents (or other adults) in learning activities at home, including ones directed toward developing skills in problem solving, critical thinking, conversation, and supervision of homework (Kellaghan and others 1993).

Broader contextual factors, such as the social and economic circumstances of the community served by the school, can also affect student learning in school. However, these factors are largely outside the control of schools. Nonetheless, obtaining support for the work of the school from local administrative and political figures is important, even in economically poor communities. Communities may become involved through support in caring for the school premises and in providing resources. Conveying the message to the community that schools provide opportunities for the development and advancement of children is particularly important; schools should clearly reflect that belief in their activities.

Planning an Intervention

When the head teacher and teachers agree on a course of action following a discussion of national assessment findings, they should draw up a plan to implement a number of strategies focused on improving student learning. The plan should specify the role of those who will be involved and should be checked from time to time to monitor implementation. For example, the plan might specify that the teacher who has the most expertise in the teaching of writing share his or her ideas with colleagues at a staff meeting. The plan should be realistic, taking into account size of school, availability of resources, abilities of individual teachers, and likelihood of support from education officials and members of the local community. Ideally, the plan should specify the following (Reezigt and Creemers 2005):

- Time needed for activities
- Priorities and order of activities
- Strategies (for example, workshops, coaching)
- Involvement of external agents and their roles and tasks, if applicable
- Staff members who will be involved and their tasks
- Role and authority of staff members who are actively involved (to prevent later misunderstandings)
- Role envisaged for students, parents, and community.

CONCLUSION

The number and complexity of the factors that affect student achievement, captured in a chart prepared by the Uganda National

Examinations Board following a series of national assessments (see figure 6.3), highlight the challenges facing schools and teachers. Professional development courses obviously have a role to play in addressing deficiencies that may be identified in teachers' subject-matter knowledge or pedagogical skills. However, other initiatives are likely to be required in schools if they are to take on board the findings of a national assessment and to react to those findings. In the case of sample-based assessments, the first challenge is to decide on the relevance of the assessment findings to individual schools. After that, if the findings are judged to be relevant, or if the school has been identified in a census-based assessment, the school is faced with the task of devising strategies that will enhance student achievement—a task that often has to be addressed with limited resources. This chapter focused on the implications of national assessment findings for teaching. If a national assessment does not identify specific courses of action, a school should be guided in developing strategies by research evidence on school effectiveness, teacher effectiveness, and the role of homes and communities in supporting student learning.

Some findings of a national assessment may point to changes in approach that are under the control of schools and teachers (for example, more time devoted to particular topics in the curriculum, more careful attention to analyzing students' homework, and more emphasis on providing feedback). Others are under the control of parents (for example, encouraging better school attendance or ensuring that homework is completed). Ministry of education officials may need to provide personnel and financial resources (a) to determine the implications of the findings of an assessment for teacher preparation and classroom practice, (b) to communicate assessment findings to schools, (c) to assist schools in interpreting findings and their relevance, (d) to assist schools in implementing strategies to address poor student achievement, and (e) to ensure that continuing support is available to schools in the implementation of strategies.

The following summary of activities, if implemented, should serve to increase the influence of a national assessment on teacher education and classroom practice:

- Involve teacher trainers in the design and implementation of the national assessment.

FIGURE 6.3

Factors That Affect Achievement: Uganda

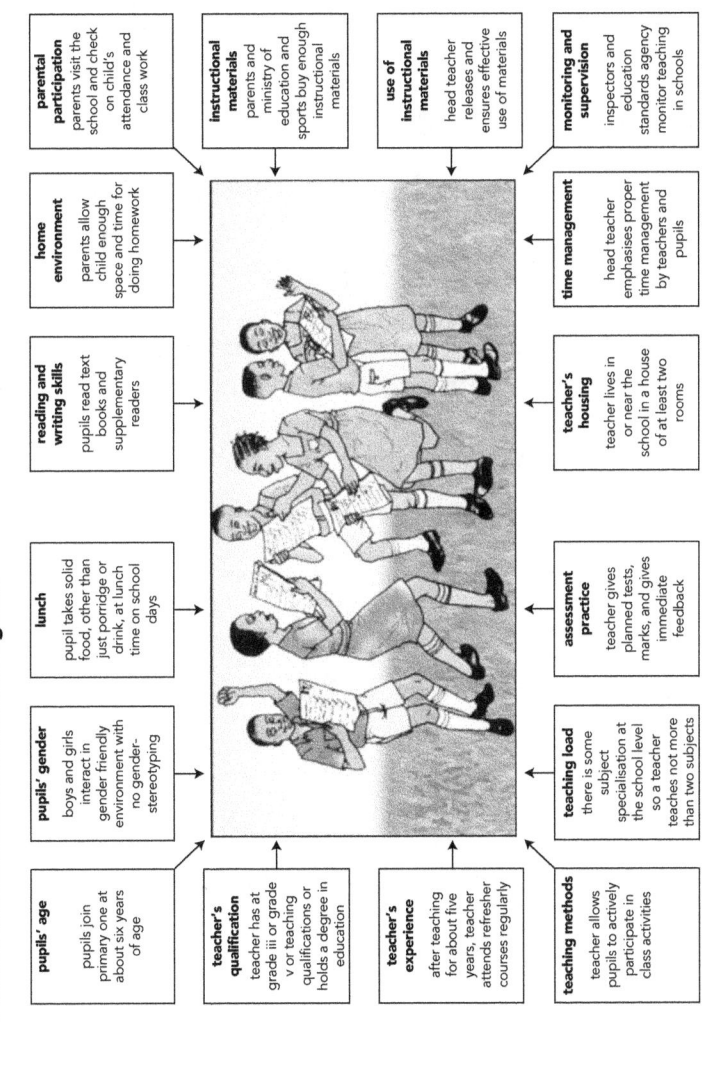

Source: Acana 2006. Reproduced with permission.

- Collect relevant information about classroom practices in questionnaires administered in the national assessment.
- Identify and report the implications of the findings of the national assessment for preservice and in-service teacher education.
- Encourage use of results by teacher trainers and preservice students.
- Prepare nontechnical, easy-to-read reports of assessment results for teachers.
- Encourage schools to review the national assessment and consider its implications.
- Advise teachers to consider school and nonschool factors that have a bearing on student performance.
- Encourage schools to increase parents' involvement in their children's education.
- Encourage schools and teachers to undertake a limited number of feasible changes in school organization and in their approaches to teaching.
- Monitor and evaluate the effects of changes that are undertaken.

CHAPTER 7

NATIONAL ASSESSMENT FINDINGS AND PUBLIC AWARENESS

Describing the performance of the education system can help focus public attention on educational concerns and stimulate national public debate. The public would undoubtedly be shocked to learn, for example, that the reading achievements of a large proportion of fifth-grade students are judged to be less than "proficient." Although politicians may sometimes find controlling the flow of this kind of information in their interest, the long-term advantages of an open information system are likely to outweigh short-term disadvantages. At its best, information about student achievements can inform debate about education, which, in turn, can contribute to increased public support for efforts to improve the system (Greaney and Kellaghan 1996; Vegas and Petrow 2008). In fact, publication of the results of a national assessment—even a sample-based one—makes the operation "high stakes" in the sense that it brings to the attention of the public information about the quality of schools, thereby raising issues of accountability (Chapman and Snyder 2000).

Whether the findings of research (including national assessments) are made openly available will be determined by political considerations and the institutional practices and culture of policy elites (see chapter 1). In some situations, authorities provide information on aggregated national (and regional) levels of achievement, but not on school- or student-level achievement. In other cases, they provide access to both types of information. In still other instances, however, authorities have resisted providing access to any kind of information. In some countries, access may be obtained by using freedom of information procedures (see box 7.1). In the absence of freedom of information legislation, governments may not consider that the public has a right to know the results of national or international assessments. Peru's Fujimori government decided against making the results of its first national assessment public for political reasons (Arregui and McLauchlan 2005). Other countries that have refused or delayed the publication of national-level results of international assessments include Mexico (Ferrer and Arregui 2003) and Romania (Gilmore 2005). A variety of reasons for withholding information have been offered, including the fear that findings might be used for interschool comparisons in the case of census assessments, that parents would not be able to understand the assessment information, and that the results were not technically adequate (Ferrer 2006).

Tradition and prior agreements with groups such as teachers' unions may limit the extent to which results are made public. In Uruguay, for example, teachers' unions, which were originally strongly opposed to the concept of a national assessment, agreed after discussions with the ministry of education on a series of steps following a census-based assessment (box 7.2) that did not promote widespread public awareness but that did succeed in providing useful information for in-service teacher training.

Special efforts may be required to attract public attention in the case of a sample-based national assessment. Certainly, this type of assessment does not attract the same media attention as an international

---

BOX 7.1

Freedom of Information Laws

Not all countries have legislation that gives the public right of access to government-held information. Only 68 of about 195 countries had freedom of information laws in 2006.

Source: Banisar 2006.

> **BOX 7.2**
>
> ### Agreements on the Release of National Assessment Results: Uruguay
>
> In Uruguay, teachers' unions agreed to the following steps to allow release of national assessment results:
>
> - National assessment results are made public in a workshop for primary school inspectors.
> - The media may attend the workshop and can receive national-level results.
> - Individual school results are not made public and are available only to inspectors and head teachers.
> - Individual parents can request school-level results from the head teacher.
> - Publishing school rankings is not permitted.
> - Results are returned to school authorities promptly (the standard is 40 days after administration).
> - Classroom teachers should not be accountable for their students' achievements.
> - Scores should be interpreted taking pertinent sociocultural factors into account.
>
> *Sources:* Benveniste 2000; Ravela 2005.

study that invites commentary on a country's performance relative to the performance of other countries, encapsulated in headlines such as "Sweden at the Level of Developing Countries" (Husén 1987) and "SA [South African] Pupils Rank Last in Maths, Science Study" (Monare 2006). National census-based assessments also tend to attract more media attention than sample-based ones when information is published (which it often is) on the performance of individual schools.

EXAMPLES OF THE USE OF ASSESSMENT RESULTS TO INFORM THE PUBLIC

Ministries of education increasingly recognize the importance of disseminating the results of national assessments. They recognize that the findings of an assessment can serve an "enlightenment" function, not just for policy and decision makers (see chapter 5) but also for the public, in identifying and thinking about problems in education. In Latin America, informing the public about student achievement levels has come to be regarded as an important outcome of a national assessment (Arregui and McLauchlan 2005). In Argentina, using student achievement results, the national government set out to provide the public with evidence that the education system was in crisis—a crisis that required the wide-sweeping reforms contained in federal law (Benveniste 2002).

In Chile, where national assessment results are used to create support networks in civil society, the annual publication of results has contributed to making education an issue on the public agenda (Benveniste 2002). Again in Chile, publicity about the association between students' socioeconomic status and their achievements increased the social demand for equity. More concretely, it formed the basis for policies focused on addressing inequities in the education system (Meckes and Carrasco 2006).

In other parts of the world, national assessment teams go to considerable length to inform the public about an assessment, sometimes in great detail. In both England and the United States, for example, although assessment strategies differ radically, extensive Web sites about assessment programs are available. Governments in both countries use Web sites to support their assessment policies and to inform the public about the quality of education. The sample-based Web site for the U.S. National Assessment of Educational Progress (http://nces.ed.gov/nationsreportcard) includes information about current and past national assessments; a section targeted to parents; details of subjects assessed, including subject frameworks; the assessment schedule; and sample items (see box 3.6). The guide for parents provides information on how students are selected for the assessment and how much time the test takes, and it states that information about individual students and schools is not reported. The Web site for the census-based assessment in England (http://www.direct.gov.uk/en/Parents/Schoolslearninganddevelopment/ExamsTestsAndTheCurriculum/) describes tests and teacher assessments.

Consistent implementation of national assessments, together with regular publication of results, is likely to raise public awareness (Meckes and Carrasco 2006). Commentary by significant figures on assessment findings is also likely to enhance public awareness. In the United States, following the release of Trends in International Mathematics and Science Study Repeat results for eighth-grade students, the U.S. secretary of education observed, "We cannot expect to lead the world in math and science if our geometry students are being taught by history teachers and our chemistry students are being taught by physical education teachers" (Riley 2000). Although the comments followed an international assessment, they are firmly rooted in observations of the national scene and could as easily have been prompted by a national assessment.

THE ROLE OF THE MEDIA

The media are an important source of information on national assessments for the public. In Germany, newspapers played a significant role in arousing public and policy-level interest following analysis of the country's performance in the Programme for International Student Assessment (PISA). Within one month of the release of the PISA 2000 results, German newspapers had devoted an estimated 687 pages to the topic, a much higher figure than that recorded for other countries (OECD and INES Project, Network A 2004). Although the study of interest was international, the findings were used to identify major unexpected achievement differences between the 16 states (*Länder*) within the country, prompting debate on the role of education provided in German schools. Results were also interpreted as providing evidence of social inequity. Public and political reaction led to reforms that included introducing common standards and measures across all *Länder*, preparing a common annual report on education in the country, and increasing the number of hours of schooling (Rubner 2006).

Although the media have an important role to play in disseminating findings, problems can be anticipated with the way the media report findings. Some reporters of national (and international) assessments seem more interested in findings that reflect badly on the education system than in findings that reflect positively. Others seek to sensationalize or distort aspects of findings. A further potential problem with the media is that studies of poor quality can attract as much attention as studies of good quality. Thus, studies carried out in a handful of schools (or even in one school) may be accorded the same seriousness as studies based on representative samples of students.

In some respects, the coverage of national assessment topics in the media has become more sophisticated over time. Instead of percentage scores, results are now more likely to be reported in terms of student proficiency levels (for example, "adequate," "proficient," "superior"). Achievement trends are reported where appropriate, and results may be categorized by region, gender, and socioeconomic status.

DEVELOPING A COMMUNICATION STRATEGY

A procedure to ensure that national assessment findings have maximum influence requires a communication strategy involving several steps (see box 7.3).

Because national assessment systems produce thousands of individual findings, the first step in developing a communication strategy

---

BOX 7.3

Procedures to Maximize the Impact of National Assessment Findings

Following a communication strategy, such as that given below, can help maximize the impact of a national assessment:

- Reach agreement on a limited number of key messages that will be consistently conveyed by official spokespersons.
- Anticipate questions and draft standard answers.
- Anticipate how journalists and interest groups will attempt to distort key messages, and devise strategies to deal with this problem.
- Develop mechanisms to monitor public and private coverage of study results, to adjust the intended message where appropriate, and to respond to misuse when it occurs.
- Develop strategies to deal with distorted interpretations of findings.

Source: Authors' compilation.

may seem somewhat anomalous: boil down all those findings into a few key messages that can be consistently conveyed to all spokespersons and that will be embedded in all summary documents, such as press releases. Properly conceived and executed, the dissemination strategy will alert target audiences to the availability of information about the national assessment and encourage them to find out more. The goal of the strategy is careful management of first impressions of the national assessment results.

Assuming that interest has been aroused, the next step is to ensure that targeted audiences get clear, nontechnical answers to any questions they may have about the meaning of key findings and to standard journalistic questions: who, what, when, where, why, how, and how much? Answers should be prepared, vetted for technical correctness, reviewed by nontechnical individuals for clarity, and rehearsed by all official spokespersons prior to release.

National study teams also need to anticipate how journalists and interest groups will attempt to distort key messages to serve their own interests. Journalists may attempt to lure spokespersons into drawing unsubstantiated conclusions or value judgments about the findings. To anticipate this possibility, official spokespersons should undergo media training, if possible, and participate in mock interviews with a colleague acting as a "hostile" journalist.

Key messages should be crafted in a way that prevents interest groups and journalists from making claims that cannot be supported by the findings. If a national study team is asked to comment on third-party statements in an effort to set up conflict, the safest course is to refrain from commenting on others' interpretation of findings and to use the occasion to reiterate key messages. The one exception is when third parties, either journalists or interest groups, make errors of fact. In these cases, the national study team must react as quickly as possible.

Reacting to incorrect interpretations presupposes that a mechanism is in place by which one can track responses to the study. National study teams actually have to put two parallel systems in place: one to monitor public coverage of the study and a second to monitor private coverage.

Public coverage can be monitored in several ways. In many countries, one can purchase the services of a clipping service that scans key media for mention and provides details in a report. A lower-cost alternative is to have members of the team keep track themselves.

Monitoring private coverage is more difficult but is often more important. It is best accomplished through personal communication with a few key users, by telephone or in person, so that one gets candid responses. Making a list of problems that arise is useful. These lists should be collated and discussed at regular intervals—very frequently in the period immediately following the release of key products and less frequently later on. The goal of the review is to decide how key messages need to be adjusted and to deal proactively and rapidly with errors of fact. National assessment managers should nominate an individual to manage this activity.

CONCLUSION

National assessment findings are generally recognized as having the potential to inform public opinion, to raise consciousness about educational matters, and to increase support for efforts to improve the education system. Nevertheless, for a number of reasons, countries still vary in the extent of their efforts to convey assessment results to the public. First, the tradition in a country may favor a closed rather than an open approach to making public information obtained by a government agency. Second, an assessment may be designed primarily to provide information for education managers and teachers, not the public. And third, lack of dissemination may reflect no more than a lack of interest, the lack of an implementation plan, or a failure at the outset to budget for dissemination.

Even when assessment findings are disseminated, they may fail in their purpose to inform public opinion because reports are too technical in nature, too dense with statistical results, or generally unintelligible to the public. When national assessment findings are distributed to the media, individual writers and editors will play a major role in determining the issues and the content that are published and ultimately in determining how the public and policy makers interpret the findings (Stack 2006). A review of the newspaper coverage of the U.S. National Assessment of Educational Progress for the period from 1990 to 1998

> **BOX 7.4**
>
> ### Brochure Cover for National Assessment, Ethiopia
>
> **HIGHLIGHTS ON ETHIOPIAN THIRD NATIONAL LEARNING ASSESSMENT (ETNLA)**
>
> The Ethiopian Third National Learning Assessment was carried out in 1999 E.C. (2006/2007) academic year on Grade 4 & 8 students across the nation in all the regions. Over 500 schools and about 23,000 students and their teachers participated in the study. This is a bird's eye view of the project related to the purpose, design, and major findings.
>
>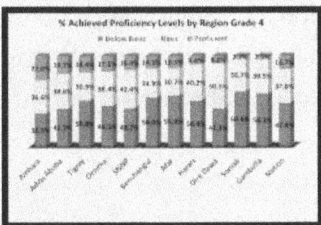
>
> **OVERVIEW**
>
> The main objectives of the two studies were to provide information about the overall learning attainments of Grade Four and Grade Eight students and to identify the major factors that potentially influence academic achievement. To achieve these objectives, both quantitative and qualitative research approaches were used. The current study used more or less similar instruments and procedures with the Ethiopian Second National Learning Assessment. In Grade Four a total of 11,373 sample students from 305 schools in all regions participated in the study. In Grade Eight a total of 10,806 sample students from 280 schools in all regions were involved. For the purpose of generating data on factors which determine the academic achievement 832 teachers and 305 school principals were included in Grade Four. And in Grade Eight 1,242 teachers and 280 school principals were involved. In the qualitative study, 312 students, 311 teachers and 286 parents participated in focus group discussions.
>
> **PURPOSE OF THE STUDY**
>
> 1. Determining grade 4 pupils' academic achievement in English, mathematics, environmental science and reading in mother tongue;
> 2. Determine grade 8 pupils' academic achievement in English, mathematics, biology, chemistry and physics;
> 3. Assessing pupils' attitude towards some of the affective factors of the education system; and
> 4. Providing policy-makers and stakeholders the findings and recommendations of grade 4 and 8 pupils' academic achievements in the subjects tested.
>
> *Source:* Ethiopia Education Quality Assurance and Examinations Agency 2007. Reproduced with permission.

suggests that newspapers tended (a) to rely heavily on the information in the press release, (b) to focus on a number of points in depth rather than present a general coverage of issues, (c) to present state rankings, (d) to use charts and graphs, (e) to have little interest in issues of test validity, and (f) to have problems understanding and communicating concepts relating to reading levels and some statistical terms (for example, statistical significance, percentiles) (Hambleton and Meara 2000).

Because having those responsible for the dissemination of national assessment findings anticipate media problems is important, focused press releases should be prepared and assessment personnel should be available for interviews. To help prevent simplistic interpretations, such as ones that attribute achievement to a single variable (for example, class size, attending a private school, time spent watching television), the national assessment team should spell out the limitations of the data.

In the future, public access to national assessment results is likely to improve through media briefings, the use of other forms of public presentation, and the production of videos and dedicated Web sites. A wide variety of media is available for this purpose, including national and local newspapers, parliamentary debates, magazine articles, brochures, radio programs, and television programs (see, for example, box 7.4). Teacher publications, seminars, and meetings, as well as newsletters, brochures, journals, and conferences, can meet the needs of special interest groups, such as teachers.

CHAPTER 8

TOWARD OPTIMIZING THE USE AND VALUE OF NATIONAL ASSESSMENTS

This book's review of the uses of the findings of a national assessment shows that assessments in many countries have provided empirical evidence about the extent to which education systems have been successful in doing what they are designed to do: foster the development of all students and provide the foundation knowledge and skills that they will require in their future educational careers and beyond. By describing how achievement is distributed in the education system, national assessments have also raised issues about the extent to which fundamental principles related to access, quality, efficiency, and equity govern the operation of the system. They did so by providing evidence about the extent that general achievement levels fall below expectations; about the failure of many students to acquire basic competencies after several years of education; and about differences in achievement associated with students' gender, place of residence, and home circumstances. Furthermore, the shift in focus from inputs to outcomes in considering the quality of education serves to draw to the attention of not just the educational community, but also politicians and the public, the importance of ensuring that students learn as a result of their educational experience.

From a perusal of the reports of national assessments throughout the world, a reasonable conclusion would be that the level of achievements revealed in the assessments is not considered satisfactory. Nevertheless, some countries take no remedial action following an assessment. In other countries, some action has been taken, including provision of resources and professional development opportunities for teachers. In a few countries, sanctions have been attached to student performance, despite the likely undesirable, if unintended, consequences associated with the practice. Devising an appropriate response to the findings of a national assessment remains a major challenge for policy makers and education managers throughout the world.

Given the complexity of the procedures (political and technical) that are required, the difficulty of responding appropriately to the findings of a national assessment is not surprising. Action may be indicated at several levels of the education system: government policy makers, central (regional and local) administrations, schools, and classroom teachers. More specific challenges can also be identified. Issues remain in many countries about the quality of national assessment data and, thus, of the reliance that can be placed on findings. Either the capacity or the political will to use assessment findings—or both—may be lacking. Assessment findings may not be communicated to stakeholders, and even when they are, they may not influence policy and decision making at the macro level or classroom practice at the micro level. Some, if not all, of these problems may reasonably be attributed to the noninvolvement of key policy makers in the design of the assessment, to the novelty of national assessments, to a lack of the technical skills that are required to execute an assessment (skills that are in scarce supply in a great many countries), and to a lack of capacity in schools to respond to the challenges posed by national assessment findings.

This chapter provides a list of the tasks (which can be used as a checklist) that need to be undertaken in a national assessment to optimize the use of findings. Then the chapter describes nine ways that future national assessment activities could be modified or expanded to describe student achievements, which, in turn, should provide a more secure basis for policy and decision making.

OPTIMIZING THE USE OF NATIONAL ASSESSMENT FINDINGS

This book's review of national assessment experiences suggests that, to optimize findings, ministry of education policy makers and managers should pay close attention to the following tasks:

Mission

- Provide from the outset clarity on the purpose of a national assessment—which is to obtain information on the outcomes of the education system as represented by student achievements with a view toward the following:
  — Informing policy and practice
  — Improving the quality of student learning with a focus on the development of higher-level cognitive skills (involving reasoning, the ability to identify and solve problems, and the ability to perform nonroutine tasks), taking account of the needs of an information-based and globally competitive economy
  — Identifying problems in the current system of educational provision and ways to address them.

Context for Use

- Develop institutional capacity to absorb and use the information provided by a national assessment.
- Integrate national assessments into existing structures, policy and decision-making processes, and channels of resource allocation.
- Create an awareness that national assessments provide information that can be used to improve the quality of student learning.

Execution of a National Assessment

- Involve policy and decision makers and other stakeholders in the design of a national assessment to ensure that it addresses their concerns.

- Ensure that those responsible for the technical aspects of a national assessment have the relevant competencies related to instrument development, sampling, analysis, and report writing.
- Ensure that those responsible for the administration of a national assessment in schools follow correct procedures.

Description of Findings

- Describe student achievement in sufficient detail to meet the needs of potential users, with a focus on diagnosing problems in the education system.
- Identify factors that are associated with high or low achievement.

Communication of Findings

- Provide information about student achievement to politicians, policy makers, and education managers in a timely fashion and in a form that is intelligible to them, and motivate them to incorporate the evidence obtained in an assessment into their policy formation and decision making.
- Provide separate reports of a national assessment that are tailored to the needs of potential users (curriculum development authorities; supervisors, inspectors, and advisers; teacher trainers; textbook writers; schools; teachers).
- Provide information on the findings of a national assessment to the media and the public.

Formulation of Policy and Programs or Interventions

- Involve stakeholders in the study of assessment findings, in setting priorities for policy and program formulation with a focus on student learning, and in devising strategies to reflect that policy, taking into account other relevant evidence (for example, the findings of educational research studies and the judgments of school inspectors, advisers, and supervisors).

- In the formulation of policy, take into account values, pressures, and constraints imposed by vested interests and make use of existing structures in the education system (for example, a mechanism for management to negotiate with trade unions) to achieve consensus or compromise in identifying courses of action.

Implementation of Policy and Programs or Interventions

- Develop criteria for the selection of schools or population groups for special support based on national assessment findings, and work with the schools and communities involved to develop programs and strategies to improve student learning.
- Take account of "best practice" in devising interventions (for example, best practice in providing in-service education for teachers).
- Identify agents to implement programs or interventions devised following a national assessment, and describe their tasks (for example, inspectors, in-service advisers, school principals).
- Provide continuing support to personnel involved in the development and implementation of strategies designed to address problems identified in an assessment.

Monitoring of Effects

- Monitor policy changes and interventions to determine if they have affected student learning.

DEVELOPING NATIONAL ASSESSMENTS TO INCREASE THEIR VALUE

This section describes nine ways that national assessment activities could be modified or enhanced to increase their value to users.

More Detailed Information about Achievement

As noted in chapter 1, one of the purposes of a national assessment is to provide evidence of particular strengths and weaknesses in students' knowledge and skills; however, the number of items in the tests used in many national assessments is too small to allow the estimation of performance in specific domains of achievement. To increase the number of items for which an assessment will obtain data without overburdening individual students, many national (and international) assessments use a rotated booklet design (Beaton 1994). Several designs are available, but the essential features of each are (a) that the test each student takes includes only a portion of all the items used in the assessment and (b) that the inclusion of common items across booklets allows student performance on each test to be linked to a common scale.

National assessment administrators, especially in the early years of operation of the assessment, may prefer that all students respond to the same test booklet and may be reluctant to use a rotated booklet design because of the complexities involved in preparing and administering assessment instruments and in doing analyses. However, in the interest of providing more detailed information on achievement, it is something toward which they should aspire as they acquire experience.

Information about Student Characteristics Associated with Student Achievement

Some national (and international) assessments have collected information on student characteristics associated with achievement in curriculum areas. For example, data were collected in Chile's national assessment on students' self-concept, attitudes toward school and learning, and peer and social relations. However, the data were not considered very useful, and the practice was discontinued (Himmel 1996).

Chapter 1 referred to the difficulty of obtaining reliable estimates of such variables, as well as problems in establishing the direction of causality between them and measures of scholastic achievement. Nevertheless, recent studies have been successful in identifying variables assessing students' learning strategies (for example, self-regulation, self-confidence, engagement, and motivation) (see Artelt and others 2003; Postlethwaite 2004a), which have been found to be significantly related to student achievement in scholastic areas. These variables merit greater consideration in national assessments that strive to identify important correlates of learning.

Information on Learning Conditions in Classrooms

Most national assessments collect background data on students' school and extra-school experiences. In some cases, data of doubtful relevance are collected; in others, analysis does not fully exploit the data. In most cases, the most significant aspects of students' experience for their school learning are not identified.

The effect of a national assessment would be enhanced if greater care were exercised in designing background questionnaires: for example, if the needs of potential users of information were identified and, in particular, if greater attention were given to obtaining information on classroom practice (see the teacher questionnaires on the CD attached to Anderson and Morgan 2008, volume 2 in this series). To date, for example, measures of content coverage in teaching (opportunity to learn), which have contributed to the explanation of student achievement in international studies, have not received a great deal of attention in national assessments.

Identification of Schools for Intervention Following a National Assessment

The problem of identifying low-performing schools on the basis of a sample-based national assessment has caused policy makers in some countries to consider moving to a census-based assessment. The issue has particular relevance in countries where a national assessment was introduced to provide information on student learning following the abolition of a public examination at the end of primary schooling. Expansion of a national assessment to include all (or most) schools and students would effectively involve assigning to the assessment some of the functions of a public examination. Before going down that road, ministry officials should seriously consider the complexities and additional costs involved in a census-based assessment and, in particular, the effects that could be anticipated if sanctions were to be attached to school, teacher, or student performance. Officials should also consider alternatives, including the development of the capacity of education personnel (especially inspectors, advisers, or supervisors) to identify schools in need of assistance. More formal procedures than are used currently in many countries would probably be required, involving, for example, testing of students (using standardized tests if available) by teachers and use of standardized rating scales by supervisory personnel.

Secondary Analyses

The initial reports of a national assessment will be prepared under time pressure. Furthermore, to be intelligible to clients, the models and methods of analysis may be less complex than those used in more basic research. For whatever reason, the richness of data that a national assessment can provide is unlikely to be fully exploited. Clearly, in this situation, making the data available for further analyses has many potential advantages (see chapter 3). Ideally, secondary analyses should be anticipated in the design of an assessment.

Use of a Longitudinal Data Collection Design in a National Assessment

In many national assessments, background data (for example, on students, their schools, and their homes and communities) are collected at the same time as data on student achievements. This approach has two disadvantages. First, inferences about causal relationships are difficult to draw from analyses in which achievement data are related to background data. Second, the "net" impact of students' educational experiences, which represents outcomes that are directly attributable to those experiences, cannot be distinguished from the "gross" impact, which reflects, in addition to net impact, other influences on student achievement (for example, students' genetic endowment, achievement on entering school, and support and assistance received at home and in the community). These problems may be addressed (at least to some extent) if data are collected on students at more than one point in time (longitudinal data). Characteristics of individual students who were assessed at an early point in time, including students' earlier achievements and background data, are then taken into account in estimating their achievements at a later point in time to determine the "value" that the particular experiences of students in school "added" to their progress (Linn 2005b).

In national assessments in francophone Africa (Programme d'Analyse des Systèmes Educatifs de CONFEMEN, or PASEC), pupils were assessed at the beginning and at the end of the academic year to obtain an estimate of growth in their achievements. Their growth was then related to factors operating in the school (teacher training, class size, textbook availability) and outside the school (parents' education, distance the pupil had to travel to school, language of the home) (Kulpoo and Coustère 1999; Michaelowa 2001; see also Greaney and Kellaghan 2008: appendix C.2). A further feature of the PASEC studies was identification of themes of national interest (for example, existing teacher employment policies) and an attempt to assess the effect of alternative arrangements, also using longitudinal data. A number of problems with the use of "value-added" studies have been identified, such as incomplete data for students arising from dropout, transfer to other schools, absenteeism, regression to the mean in statistical analysis, and unreliability of measures when the number of students in a school is small.

Follow-Up Case Studies

Some follow-up studies have examined factors associated with high (or low) achievement in an effort to strengthen the basis for drawing causal inferences from national assessment data. In the United States, for example, the National Education Goals Panel conducted an analysis of one of the highest-scoring states (Connecticut) to identify educational policies and practices that may have contributed to high reading scores. Three policies were credited with the state's performance: (a) providing detailed information on student performance to a wide range of stakeholders (districts, schools, teachers, parents); (b) monitoring student achievement over time; and (c) providing additional resources to the neediest districts (for example, professional development for teachers; support for, and assessment of, beginning teachers) (Baron 1999).

Further information was obtained following a national assessment in mathematics (which included items from the Second International Mathematics Study of the International Association for the Evaluation of Educational Achievement) of 13- and 17-year-olds in the Dominican Republic in the wake of great concern about the poor performance of students. In this case, a study, involving classroom observation and interviews with teachers, was carried out of the teaching of mathematics in a sample of grade 8 classrooms to identify instructional and learning procedures. Problems identified were addressed by (a) setting up a curriculum development center to prepare materials to support the teaching of mathematics and (b) providing in-service programs for teachers (Luna 1992).

Caution is indicated in interpreting the performance of units with high levels of student achievement, especially when the unit is a school with a small number of students. Because any small group is likely to exhibit large swings in test scores from year to year relative to the distribution of between-school differences, any "reasons" proposed by a school for superior performance could well be spurious (Kane and Staiger 2002).

Follow-Up Experimental or Quasi-experimental Study

Experiments, which involve the manipulation and control of variables, provide the strongest basis for drawing inferences about cause-effect relationships. Their use would involve designing a study to test hypotheses about student improvement by implementing a strategy prompted by the findings of a national assessment—for example, providing additional resources to schools—in a number of schools or areas (the *treatment group*). After a set period, the effect of the strategy would be evaluated by comparing the performance of the treatment group on a measure of achievement with that of a *control group* (that is, a group of schools or areas that received no additional resources but were otherwise similar to the schools or areas in the treatment group). The best way to ensure comparability between a treatment group and a control group is to assign participants to groups randomly. Because of the practical difficulties in doing so in real-life settings, however, a quasi-experimental design that does not involve random assignment is frequently used. In this case, a comparison group is chosen to be as similar as possible to the treatment group (in particular, efforts must be made to reduce the possibility of selection bias); information on variables of interest is obtained before and after treatment; and covariance or regression analysis may be used to adjust posttreatment measures, as long as initial differences are not large.

A few randomized studies have been conducted in developing countries (India, Kenya, Nicaragua), though not in the context of a national assessment. In these studies, a treatment (for example, providing workbooks and radio instruction, textbooks, or a remedial program) was implemented in randomly selected schools, and its effect was estimated on the basis of a comparison of the achievements of students in these schools with the achievements of students in similar schools that did not receive the treatment (Glewwe and Kremer 2006).

Experiments or quasi-experiments have not been used in the context of a national assessment as far as the authors are aware. At least in part, their absence may be because they are difficult to implement and monitor. A more serious problem from the point of view of the policy or decision maker may be the cost and time that it takes to carry out a study. One can argue, however, that the costs of experiments are small compared with the costs of policies that do not work or that could have been significantly more effective if the information that can be derived from an experiment or quasi-experiment had been available (see Postlethwaite 1975). However, the planning, implementation, and analysis required in experimental or quasi-experimental studies may be beyond the capacity of many agencies that carry out a national assessment. In that case, such studies are best assigned to a more specialized research agency.

Assessment of Children Outside the Education System

Because national assessments are limited to children in the education system, they do not throw any light on unmet quantitative needs for access to the system, except in a very limited way (for example, in providing information related to the distance from school of a student's home). In many developing countries, however, large numbers of school-age children do not attend school or attend for only a short time. Given a commitment in these countries to universal primary education, knowing something about the achievements of these children; the barriers to access that they experience; their use of alternative resources (for example, nonformal education); and their unmet needs would be of value. Obtaining this information would, of course, require methods of sampling and assessment other than those currently used in school-based national assessments. India provides an example of a study in which children 6 to 16 years of age are assessed (in reading, mathematics, and English) in their homes (http://www.asercentre. org). Other models that provide data on non-school-going children exist in ad hoc studies (see, for example, Greaney, Khandker, and Alam 1999) and in the context of household surveys.

CONCLUSION

As national assessment activity becomes more securely established in education systems, the use of findings might reasonably be expected to expand. Two sets of conditions can be identified that, if met, should help to bring about this expansion. First, (a) developing the technical skills and communication strategies of those responsible for national assessments, (b) enhancing the ability of policy and decision makers to interpret assessment findings and to devise strategies to address identified shortcomings, and (c) involving a wide range of stakeholders should contribute to the establishment of a more hospitable environment for the use of findings. Second, consideration should be given to whether the kinds of information currently provided by national assessments meet the needs of users, whether procedures need to be modified, or whether supplementary studies are required to provide guidance to policy and decision makers. Meeting these conditions may require further funding and commitment. The additional expenditure would not be great in the context of the cost of carrying out a national assessment, however, and would be likely to add considerable value to the exercise.

REFERENCES

Acana, S. 2006. "Reporting Results of National Assessment: Uganda Experience." Paper presented at the 32nd Annual Conference of the International Association for Educational Assessment, Singapore, May 22–26.

———. 2008. "Using Assessment Results to Improve Learning: A Message to Headteachers." Paper presented at the 34th Annual Conference of the International Association for Educational Assessment, Cambridge, U.K., September 7–12.

Aguerrondo, I. 1992. "Educational Reform in Latin America: A Survey of Four Decades." *Prospects* 22 (3): 353–65.

Ainley, J., J. Fraillon, and C. Freeman. 2007. *National Assessment Program: ICT Literacy Years 6 and 10 Report, 2005.* Carlton South, Victoria, Australia: Ministerial Council on Education, Employment, Training and Youth Affairs. http://www.mceetya.edu.au/verve/_resources/NAP_ICTL_2005_Years_6_and_10_Report.pdf.

Altinok, N. 2008. "An International Perspective on Trends in the Quality of Learning Achievement (1965–2007)." Background paper prepared for *Overcoming Inequality: Why Governance Matters—EFA Global Monitoring Report 2009*, United Nations Educational, Scientific, and Cultural Organization, Paris. http://unesdoc.unesco.org/images/0017/001780/178009e.pdf.

Amrein, A. L., and D. C. Berliner. 2002. "High-Stakes Testing, Uncertainty, and Student Learning." *Education Policy Analysis Archives* 10 (18). http://epaa.asu.edu/epaa/v10n18/.

Anderson, P., and G. Morgan. 2008. *Developing Tests and Questionnaires for a National Assessment of Achievement.* Washington, DC: World Bank.

Anderson, S. E. 2002. "The Double Mirrors of School Improvement: The Aga Khan Foundation in East Africa." In *Improving Schools through Teacher Development: Case Studies of the Aga Khan Foundation Projects in East Africa,* ed. S. E. Anderson, 1–20. Lisse, Netherlands: Swets & Zetlinger.

Arregui, P., and C. McLauchlan. 2005. "Utilization of Large-Scale Assessment Results in Latin America." Report prepared for the Partnership for Educational Revitalization in the Americas and the World Bank Institute, Washington, DC.

Artelt, C., J. Baumert, N. Julius-McElvany, and J. Peschar. 2003. *Learners for Life: Student Approaches to Learning—Results from PISA 2000.* Paris: Organisation for Economic Co-operation and Development.

Banisar, D. 2006. *Freedom of Information around the World 2006: A Global Survey of Access to Government Records Laws.* London: Privacy International. http://www.freedominfo.org/documents/global_survey2006.pdf.

Baron, J. B. 1999. "Exploring High and Improving Achievement in Connecticut." Document 1233, National Educational Goals Panel, Washington, DC. http://govinfo.library.unt.edu/negp/issues/publication/othpress/body.pdf.

Báthory, Z. 1992. "Hungarian Experiences in International Student Achievement Surveys." *Prospects* 22 (4): 434–40.

Beaton, A. E. 1994. "Item Sampling in Testing." In *The International Encyclopedia of Education,* 2nd ed., ed. T. Husén and T. N. Postlethwaite, 3055–61. Oxford, U.K.: Pergamon.

Beaton, A. E., and N. L. Allen. 1992. "Interpreting Scales through Scale Anchoring." *Journal of Educational Statistics* 17 (2): 191–204.

Beaton, A. E., and E. G. Johnson. 1992. "Overview of the Scaling Methodology Used in the National Assessment." *Journal of Educational Measurement* 29 (2): 163–75.

Benveniste, L. 2000. "Student Assessment as a Political Construction: The Case of Uruguay." *Education Policy Analysis Archives* 8 (32). http://epaa.asu.edu/epaa/v8n32.html.

———. 2002. "The Political Structuration of Assessment: Negotiating State Power and Legitimacy." *Comparative Education Review* 46 (1): 89–118.

Bernard, J. M., and K. Michaelowa. 2006. "How Can Countries Use Cross-National Research Results to Address 'the Big Policy Issues'?" In *Cross-National Studies of the Quality of Education: Planning Their Design and*

Managing Their Impact, ed. K. N. Ross and I. J. Genevois, 229–40. Paris: International Institute for Educational Planning.

Bethell, G., and R. Mihail. 2005. "Assessment and Examinations in Romania." *Assessment in Education* 12 (1): 77–96.

Bhutan Board of Examinations. 2004. *National Educational Assessment in Bhutan: A Benchmark of Student Achievement in Literacy at Class 5, 2003*. Thinphu: Ministry of Education.

Binkley, M., and K. Rust, eds. 1994. *Reading Literacy in the United States: Technical Report of the U.S. Component of the IEA Reading Literacy Study*. Washington, DC: Office of Educational Research and Improvement, U.S. Department of Education.

Blalock, A. B. 1999. "Evaluation Research and the Performance Management Movement." *Evaluation* 5 (2): 117–49.

Bonnet, G. 2007. "What Do Recent Evaluations Tell Us about the State of Teachers in Sub-Saharan Africa." Background paper for *Education for All: Will We Make It—EFA Global Monitoring Report 2008*, United Nations Educational, Scientific, and Cultural Organization, Paris. http://unesdoc.unesco.org/images/0015/001555/155511e.pdf.

Braun, H. 2004. "Reconsidering the Impact of High-Stakes Testing." *Education Policy Analysis Archives* 12 (1). http://epaa.asu.edu/epaa/v2n1/.

Braun, H., A. Kanjee, E. Bettinger, and M. Kremer. 2006. *Improving Education through Assessment, Innovation, and Evaluation*. Cambridge, MA: American Academy of Arts and Sciences.

British Columbia Ministry of Education. 1999. *Interpreting Your District's Assessment Results, 1999*. Victoria: Province of British Columbia.

Brophy, J. E., and T. L. Good. 1986. "Teacher Behavior and Student Achievement." In *Third Handbook of Research on Teaching*, ed. M. Wittrock, 328–75. New York: Macmillan.

Campbell, J., D. L. Kelly, I. V. S. Mullis, M. O. Martin, and M. Sainsbury. 2001. *Framework and Specifications for PIRLS Assessment 2001*. 2nd ed. Chestnut Hill, MA: Boston College.

Campbell, J., L. Kyriakides, D. Muijs, and W. Robinson. 2004. *Assessing Teacher Effectiveness: Developing a Differentiated Model*. London: Routledge Falmer.

Carroll, D. 1996. "The Grade 3 and 5 Assessment in Egypt." In *National Assessments: Testing the System*, ed. P. Murphy, V. Greaney, M. E. Lockheed, and C. Rojas, 157–65. Washington, DC: World Bank.

Chabbott, C., and E. J. Elliott, eds. 2003. *Understanding Others, Educating Ourselves: Getting More from International Comparative Studies in Education.* Washington, DC: National Academies Press.

Chapman, D. W., and C. W. Snyder. 2000. "Can High Stakes National Testing Improve Instruction? Reexamining Conventional Wisdom." *International Journal of Educational Development* 20 (6): 457–74.

Cheng, K., and H. Yip. 2006. *Facing the Knowledge Society: Reforming Secondary Education in Hong Kong and Shanghai.* Washington, DC: World Bank.

Clegg, S. R., and T. F. Clarke. 2001. "Intelligence: Organizational." In *International Encyclopedia of the Social and Behavioral Sciences*, vol. 11, ed. N. J. Smelser and P. B. Baltes, 7665–70. Amsterdam: Elsevier.

Clotfelter, C. T., and H. L. Ladd. 1996. "Recognizing and Rewarding Success in Public Schools." In *Holding Schools Accountable: Performance-Based Reform in Education*, ed. H. F. Ladd, 23–63. Washington, DC: Brookings Institution.

DataAngel Policy Research. 2007. *A Tool for Understanding Performance in Science Instruction in Qatar.* Doha: Supreme Education Council.

Davies, I. C. 1999. "Evaluation and Performance Management in Government." *Evaluation* 5 (2): 150–59.

de Vise, D. 2005. "State Gains Not Echoed in Federal Testing: Results Fuel Criticism of Md., Va. Education." *Washington Post*, October 24, B01.

Duthilleul, Y., and R. Allen. 2005. "Which Teachers Make a Difference? Implications for Policy Makers in SACMEQ Countries." Paper presented at the Educational Policy Research Conference, International Institute for Educational Planning, Paris, September 28–30.

Eivers, E., G. Shiel, R. Perkins, and J. Cosgrove. 2005a. *Succeeding in Reading? Reading Standards in Irish Primary Schools.* Dublin: Department of Education and Science.

———. 2005b. *The 2004 National Assessment of English Reading.* Dublin: Educational Research Centre.

Elley, W. B. 1992. *How in the World Do Students Read? IEA Study of Reading Literacy.* The Hague, Netherlands: International Association for the Evaluation of Educational Achievement.

Elmore, R., and D. Burney. 1999. "Investing in Teacher Training." In *Teaching as the Learning Profession*, ed. L. Darling-Hammond and G. Sykes, 236–91. San Francisco, CA: Jossey-Bass.

Ethiopia Education Quality Assurance and Examinations Agency. 2007. *Highlights of the Findings: Ethiopian Third National Learning Assessment.* Addis Ababa: Ethiopia Education Quality Assurance and Examinations Agency.

Ferrer, G. 2006. *Educational Assessment Systems in Latin America: Current Practice and Future Challenges.* Washington, DC: Partnership for Educational Revitalization in the Americas.

Ferrer, G., and P. Arregui. 2003. "Las Pruebas Internacionales de Aprendizaje en América Latina y Su Impacto en la Calidad de la Educación: Criterio para Guiar Futuras Aplicaciones." Documento de Trabajo 26, Partnership for Educational Revitalization in the Americas, Santiago.

Finn, J. D., and C. M. Achilles. 1990. "Tennessee's Class Size Study: Findings, Implications, Misconceptions." *Educational Evaluation and Policy Analysis* 21 (2): 97–110.

Forster, M. 2001. *A Policy Maker's Guide to Systemwide Assessment Programs.* Camberwell, Victoria: ACER Press.

Frederiksen, J., and A. Collins. 1989. "A Systems Approach to Educational Testing." *Educational Researcher* 18 (9): 27–32.

Fullan, M. 2001. *The New Meaning of Educational Change.* New York: Teachers College Press.

Fuller, B. 1987. "What School Factors Raise Achievement in the Third World?" *Review of Educational Research* 57 (3): 255–92.

Garet, M. S., A. C. Porter, L. Desimone, B. F. Birman, and K. S. Yoon. 2001. "What Makes Professional Development Effective? Results from a National Sample of Teachers." *American Educational Research Journal* 38 (4): 915–45.

Gebrekidan, Z. 2006. "Ethiopian Second National Learning Assessment." Paper presented at the National Assessment Capacity Building Workshop, Using National Assessment Results, Kampala, January 30–February 2.

Georgia Department of Education. n.d. "Standards, Instruction, and Assessment." Georgia Department of Education, Atlanta. http://www.doe.k12.ga.us/ci_testing.aspx? Page Req = C1_TESTING_NAEP.

Gilmore, A. 2005. "The Impact of PIRLS (2001) and TIMSS (2003) in Low and Middle-Income Countries: An Evaluation of the Value of World Bank Support for International Surveys of Reading Literacy (PIRLS) and Mathematics and Science (TIMSS)." International Association for the Evaluation of Educational Achievement, Amsterdam. http://www.iea.nl/fileadmin/user_upload/docs/WB_report.pdf.

Glewwe, P., and M. Kremer. 2006. "Schools, Teachers, and Education Outcomes in Developing Countries." In *Handbook of the Economics of Education*, vol. 2, ed. E. A. Hanushek and F. Welch, 945–1017. Amsterdam: Elsevier.

Goldstein, H. 1983. "Measuring Changes in Educational Attainment over Time: Problems and Possibilities." *Journal of Educational Measurement* 20 (4): 369–77.

González, E. J. 2002. *Evaluation Systems in Latin America*. Brasília: National Institute for Educational Studies and Research, Ministry of Education.

González, P., A. Mizala, and P. Romaguera. 2002. "Recursos Diferenciados a la Educación Subvencionada en Chile." Serie Economía 150, Centro de Economía Aplicada, Departamento de Ingeniería Industrial, Facultad de Ciencies Físicas y Matemáticas, Universidad de Chile, Santiago.

Grant, S., P. Peterson, and A. Shojgreen-Downer. 1996. "Learning to Teach Mathematics in the Context of System Reform." *American Educational Research Journal* 33 (2): 500–43.

Greaney, V., and T. Kellaghan. 1996. *Monitoring the Learning Outcomes of Education Systems*. Washington, DC: World Bank.

———. 2008. *Assessing National Achievement Levels in Education*. Washington, DC: World Bank.

Greaney, V., S. R. Khandker, and M. Alam. 1999. *Bangladesh: Assessing Basic Learning Skills*. Dhaka: University Press.

Griffith, J. E., and E. A. Medrich. 1992. "What Does the United States Want to Learn from International Comparative Studies in Education?" *Prospects* 22 (4): 476–84.

Gucwa, B., and M. Mastie. 1989. "Pencils Down!" Michigan State Board of Education, Lansing. http://www.ncrel.org/sdrs/areas/issues/methods/assment/as6penc2.htm.

Guilfoyle, C. 2006. "NCLB: Is There Life Beyond Testing?" *Educational Leadership* 64 (3): 8–13.

Gvirtz, S., and S. Larripa. 2004. "National Evaluation System in Argentina: Problematic Present and Uncertain Future." *Assessment in Education* 11 (3): 349–64.

Haertel, E. H., and J. L. Herman. 2005. "A Historical Perspective on Validity Arguments for Accountability Testing." In *Uses and Misuses of Data for Educational Accountability and Improvement: The 104th Yearbook of the National Society for the Study of Education, Part 2*, ed. J. L. Herman and E. H. Haertel, 1–34. Malden, MA: Blackwell.

Hambleton, R. K, and K. Meara. 2000. "Newspaper Coverage of NAEP Results, 1990 to 1998." In *Student Performance Standards on the National Assessment of Educational Progress: Affirmations and Improvements*, ed. M. L. Bourque and S. Byrd, 131–55. Washington, DC: National Assessment Governing Board.

Hambleton, R. K., and S. C. Slater. 1997. "Are NAEP Executive Summary Reports Understandable to Policy Makers and Stakeholders?" CSE Technical Report 430, Center for the Study of Evaluation, National Center for Research on Evaluation, Standards, and Student Testing, Los Angeles, CA.

Himmel, E. 1996. "National Assessment in Chile." In *National Assessments: Testing the System*, ed. P. Murphy, V. Greaney, M. E. Lockheed, and C. Rojas, 111–28. Washington, DC: World Bank.

Hopmann, S. T., and G. Brinek. 2007. "Introduction: PISA According to PISA—Does PISA Keep What It Promises?" In *PISA Zufolge PISA: PISA According to PISA*, ed. S. T. Hopmann, G. Brinek, and M. Retzl, 9–19. Vienna: LIT.

Howie, S. 2002. "English Proficiencies and Contextual Factors Influencing Mathematics Achievements of Secondary School Pupils in South Africa." PhD thesis, University of Twente, Enschede, Netherlands.

Howie, S., and T. Plomp. 2005. "International Comparative Studies of Education and Large-Scale Change." In *International Handbook of Education Policy*, ed. N. Bascia, A. Cumming, A. Datnow, K. Leithword, and D. Livingstone, 75–99. Dordrecht, Netherlands: Springer.

Husén, T. 1984. "Issues and Their Background." In *Educational Research and Policy: How Do They Relate?* ed. T. Husén and M. Kogan, 1–36. Oxford, U.K.: Pergamon.

———. 1987. "Policy Impact of IEA Research." *Comparative Education Review* 31 (1): 29–46.

Kane, T. J., and D. O. Staiger. 2002. "Volatility in School Test Scores: Implications for Test-Based Accountability Systems." In *Brookings Papers on Education Policy, 2002*, ed. D. Ravitch, 235–83. Washington, DC: Brookings Institution Press.

Kellaghan, T., and V. Greaney. 1992. *Using Examinations to Improve Education: A Study in Fourteen African Countries*. Washington, DC: World Bank.

———. 2001. *Using Assessment to Improve the Quality of Education*. Paris: International Institute for Educational Planning.

———. 2004. *Assessing Student Learning in Africa*. Washington, DC: World Bank.

Kellaghan, T., and G. F. Madaus. 2000. "Outcome Evaluation." In *Evaluation Models: Viewpoints on Educational and Human Services Evaluation*, 2nd ed., ed. D. L. Stufflebeam, G. F. Madaus, and T. Kellaghan, 97–112. Boston: Kluwer Academic.

Kellaghan, T., K. Sloane, B. Alvarez, and B. S. Bloom. 1993. *The Home Environment and School Learning*. San Francisco, CA: Jossey-Bass.

Kirsch, I., J. De Jong, D. Lafontaine, J. McQueen, J. Mendelovits, and C. Monseur. 2002. *Reading for Change: Performance and Engagement across Countries—Results from PISA 2000*. Paris: Organisation for Economic Co-operation and Development.

Kulm, G., J. Roseman, and M. Treistman. 1999. "A Bench-Based Approach to Textbook Evaluation." *Science Books and Films* 35 (4): 147–53.

Kulpoo, D., and P. Coustère. 1999. "Developing National Capacities for Assessment and Monitoring through Effective Partnerships." In *Partnerships for Capacity Building and Quality Improvements in Education: Papers from the ADEA 1997 Biennial Meeting, Dakar*. Paris: Association for the Development of Education in Africa.

Kupermintz, H., M. M. Ennis, L. S. Hamilton, J. E. Talbert, and R. E. Snow. 1995. "Enhancing the Validity and Usefulness of Large-Scale Educational Assessments: I. NELS:88 Mathematics Achievement." *American Educational Research Journal* 32 (3): 525–54.

Kuwait Ministry of Education. 2008. *PIRLS 2006: Kuwait Technical Report*. Kuwait City: Kuwait Ministry of Education.

Leimu, K. 1992. "Interests and Modes in Research Utilisation: The Finnish IEA Experience." *Prospects* 22 (4): 425–33.

Linn, R. L. 2000. "Assessments and Accountability." *Educational Researcher* 29 (2): 4–16.

———. 2005a. "Conflicting Demands of No Child Left Behind and State Systems: Mixed Messages about School Performance." *Education Policy Analysis Archives* 13 (33). http://epaa.asu.edu/epaa/v13n33/.

———. 2005b. "Issues in the Design of Accountability Systems." In *Uses and Misuses of Data for Educational Accountability and Improvement: The 104th Yearbook of the National Society for the Study of Education, Part 2*, ed. J. L. Herman and E. H. Haertel, 78–98. Malden, MA: Blackwell.

Linn, R. L., and E. Baker. 1996. "Can Performance-Based Student Assessments Be Psychometrically Sound?" In *Performance-Based Student Assessment: Challenges and Possibilities: 95th Yearbook of the National Society for the Study of Education, Part 1*, ed. J. N. Baron and D. P. Wolf, 84–103. Chicago: National Society for the Study of Education.

Lockheed, M. E., and A. M. Verspoor. 1991. *Improving Primary Education in Developing Countries*. Oxford, U.K.: Oxford University Press.

Lovett, S. 1999. "National Education Monitoring Project: Teachers Involvement and Development—Professional Development from NEMP." Paper presented at New Zealand Association for Research in Education and Australian Association for Research in Education Conference, Melbourne, Australia, November 29–December 2.

Luna, E. 1992. "Dominican Republic: The Study on Teaching and Learning in Mathematics." *Prospects* 22 (4): 448–54.

Madamombe, R. T. 1995. "A Comment on the Analysis of Educational Research Data for Policy Development: An Example from Zimbabwe." *International Journal of Educational Research* 23 (4): 397–402.

Madaus, G. F., and T. Kellaghan. 1992. "Curriculum Evaluation and Assessment." In *Handbook of Research on Curriculum*, ed. P. W. Jackson, 119–54. New York: Macmillan.

Madaus, G. F., M. Russell, and J. Higgins. 2009. *The Paradoxes of High Stakes Testing: How They Affect Students, Their Parents, Teachers, Principals, Schools, and Society*. Charlotte, NC: Information Age Publishing.

Martin, M. O., I. V. S. Mullis, and S. J. Chrostowski. 2004. *The Trends in International Mathematics and Science Study 2003: Technical Report*. Chestnut Hill, MA: International Study Center, Boston College.

Mauritius Examinations Syndicate. 2003. *Monitoring Learning Achievement: Joint UNESCO/UNICEF Project—A Survey of 9-Year-Old Children in the Republic of Mauritius*. Reduit, Mauritius: Mauritius Examinations Syndicate.

McDonnell, L. M. 2005. "Assessment and Accountability from the Policy Maker's Perspective." In *Uses and Misuses of Data for Educational Accountability and Improvement: 104th Yearbook of the National Society for the Study of Education, Part 2*, ed. J. L. Herman and E. H. Haertel, 35–54.

McQuillan, J. 1998. "Seven Myths about Literacy in the U.S." *Practical Assessment, Research, and Evaluation* 6 (1). http://pareonline.net/getvn.asp?v=6&n=1.

Meckes, L., and R. Carrasco. 2006. "SIMCE: Lessons from the Chilean Experience in National Assessment Systems of Learning Outcomes." Paper presented at the Conference on Lessons from Best Practices in Promoting Education for All: Latin America and the Caribbean, hosted by the World Bank and the Inter-American Development Bank, Cartagena de Indias, Colombia, October 9–11.

Messick, S. 1989. "Validity." In *Educational Measurement*, 3rd ed., ed. R. Linn, 13–103. New York: American Council on Education and Macmillan.

Michaelowa, K. 2001. "Primary Education Quality in Francophone Sub-Saharan Africa: Determinants of Learning Achievement and Efficiency Considerations." *World Development* 29 (10): 1699–716.

Michaelowa, K., and A. Wechtler. 2006. *The Cost-Effectiveness of Inputs in Primary Education: Insights from the Literature and Recent Student Surveys for Sub-Saharan Africa*. Hamburg: Institute of International Economics.

Monare, M. 2006. "SA Pupils Rank Last in Maths, Science Study." *Star* (Johannesburg), December 6.

Moncada, G., R. Hernández Rodríguez, M. C. Aguilar, D. Orellana, M. Alas Solís, and B. Hernández. 2003. *Uso e Impacto de la Información Empírica en la Formulación y Ejecución de Política de Educación Básica en Honduras en el Período 1990–2002*. Tegucigalpa: Dirección de Investigación, Universidad Pedagógica Nacional Francisco Morazán.

Mullis, I. V. S., A. M. Kennedy, M. O. Martin, and M. Sainsbury. 2006. *PIRLS 2006: Assessment Framework and Specifications*. Chestnut Hill, MA: International Study Center, Boston College.

Mullis, I. V. S., M. O. Martin, E. J. González, and S. J. Chrostowski. 2004. *Findings from IEA's Trends in International Mathematics and Science Study at the Fourth and Eighth Grades*. Chestnut Hill, MA: International Study Center, Boston College.

Murimba, M. 2005. "The Impact of the Southern and Eastern Africa Consortium for Monitoring Educational Quality (SACMEQ)." *Prospects* 35 (1): 91–108.

Murphy, J., J. Yff, and N. Shipman. 2000. "Implementation of the Interstate School Leaders Licensure Consortium Standards." *International Journal of Leadership in Education* 3 (1): 17–39.

Nassor, S., and K. A. Mohammed. 1998. *The Quality of Education: Some Policy Suggestions Based on a Survey of Schools—Zanzibar*. Paris: International Institute for Educational Planning.

Nepal Educational and Developmental Service Centre. 1999. *National Assessment of Grade 5 Students*. Kathmandu: Nepal Educational and Developmental Service Centre.

Nigeria Federal Ministry of Education. 2000. *Education for All: The Year 2000 Assessment*. Abuja: Nigeria Federal Ministry of Education.

Nzomo, J., M. Kariuki, and L. Guantai. 2001. "The Quality of Education: Some Policy Suggestions Based on a Survey of Schools." Southern and Eastern Africa Consortium for Monitoring Educational Quality Policy Research Paper 6, International Institute for Educational Planning, Paris.

Nzomo, J., and D. Makuwa. 2006. "How Can Countries Move from Cross-National Research Results to Dissemination and Then to Policy Reform? Case Studies from Kenya and Namibia." In *Cross-National Studies of the Quality of Education: Planning Their Design and Managing Their Impact*, ed. K. N. Ross and I. J. Genevois, 213–28. Paris: International Institute for Educational Planning.

OECD (Organisation for Economic Co-operation and Development). 2004. *Chile: Reviews of National Policies for Education*. Paris: OECD.

OECD (Organisation for Economic Co-operation and Development) and INES (International Indicators of Education Systems) Project, Network A. 2004. "Attention Getting Results." *Review of Assessment Activities* 16 (February–March): 2.

Ogle, L. T., A. Sen, E. Pahlke, D. Jocelyn, D. Kastberg, S. Roey, and T. Williams. 2003. "International Comparisons in Fourth Grade Reading Literacy: Findings from the Progress in International Reading Literacy Study (PIRLS) of 2001." U.S. Department of Education, National Center for Education Statistics, Washington, DC. http://nces.ed.gov/pubs2003/2003073.pdf.

Olivares, J. 1996. "Sistema de Medición de la Calidad de la Educación de Chile: SIMCE—Algunos Problemas de la Medición." *Revista Iberoamericana de Educación* 10: 117–96. http://www.rieoei.org/oeivirt/rie10a07.htm.

Pérez, B. A. 2006. "Success in Implementing Education Policy Dialogue in Peru." United States Agency for International Development, Washington, DC.

Perie, M., W. Grigg, and G. Dion. 2005. "The Nation's Report Card: Mathematics 2005." National Center for Education Statistics, U.S. Department of Education, Washington, DC. http://nces.ed.gov/nationsreportcard/pdf/main2005/2006453.pdf.

Porter, A., and A. Gamoran. 2002. "Progress and Challenges for Large-Scale Studies." In *Methodological Advances in Cross-National Surveys of Educational Achievement*, ed. A. C. Porter and A. Gamoran, 3–23. Washington, DC: National Academies Press.

Postlethwaite, T. N. 1975. "The Surveys of the International Association for the Evaluation of Educational Achievement (IEA)." In *Educational Policy and International Assessment: Implications of the IEA Surveys of Achievement*, ed. A. C. Purves and D. U. Levine, 1–32. Berkeley, CA: McCutchan.

———. 1987. "Comparative Educational Achievement Research: Can It Be Improved?" *Comparative Education Review* 31 (1): 150–58.

———. 1995. "Calculation and Interpretation of Between-School and Within-School Variation in Achievement (*rho*)." In *Measuring What Students Learn*, 83–94. Paris: Organisation for Economic Co-operation and Development.

———. 2004a. *Monitoring Educational Achievements*. Paris: International Institute for Educational Planning.

———. 2004b. "What Do International Assessment Studies Tell Us about the Quality of School Systems?" Background paper for *The Quality Imperative: EFA Global Monitoring Report 2005*. United Nations Educational, Scientific, and Cultural Organization, Paris. http://unesdoc.unesco.org/images/0014/001466/146692e.pdf.

Postlethwaite, T. N., and T. Kellaghan. 2008. *National Assessments of Educational Achievement*. Paris: International Institute for Educational Planning; Brussels: International Academy of Education.

Powdyel, T. S. 2005. "The Bhutanese Education Assessment Experience: Some Reflections." *Prospects* 35 (1): 45–57.

Pravalpruk, K. 1996. "National Assessment in Thailand." In *National Assessments: Testing the System*, ed. P. Murphy, V. Greaney, M. E. Lockheed, and C. Rojas, 137–45. Washington, DC: World Bank.

Ravela, P. 2002. "Cómo Presentan Sus Resultados los Sistemas Nacionales de Evaluación Educativa en América Latina?" Partnership for Educational Revitalization in the Americas, Washington, DC.

———. 2005. "A Formative Approach to National Assessments: The Case of Uruguay." *Prospects* 35 (1): 21–43.

———. 2006. "Using National Assessments to Improve Teaching … and Learning: The Experience of UMRE in Uruguay." Paper presented at the Conference on Lessons from Best Practices in Promoting Education for All: Latin America and the Caribbean, hosted by the World Bank and the Inter-American Development Bank, Cartagena de Indias, Colombia, October 9–11.

Reezigt, G. J., and B. P. M. Creemers. 2005. "A Comprehensive Framework for Effective School Improvement." *School Effectiveness and School Improvement* 16 (4): 407–24.

Reimers, F. 2003. "The Social Context of Educational Evaluation in Latin America." In *International Handbook of Educational Evaluation*, ed. T. Kellaghan and D. L. Stufflebeam, 441–63. Boston: Kluwer Academic.

Reynolds, D. 2000. "School Effectiveness: The International Dimension." In *The International Handbook of School Effectiveness Research*, ed. C. Teddlie and D. Reynolds, 232–56. London: Falmer.

Reynolds, D., and C. Teddlie. 2000. "The Processes of School Effectiveness." In *The International Handbook of School Effectiveness Research*, ed. C. Teddlie and D. Reynolds, 134–59. London: Falmer.

Riley, R. W. 2000. Remarks prepared for a TIMSS-R press conference, Washington, DC, December 5. http://www.ed.gov/Speeches/12-2000/120500.html.

Robertson, I. 2005. "Issues Relating to Curriculum, Policy, and Gender Raised by National and International Surveys of Achievement in Mathematics." *Assessment in Education* 12 (3): 217–36.

Robitaille, D. F., A. E. Beaton, and T. Plomp, eds. 2000. *The Impact of TIMSS on the Teaching and Learning of Mathematics and Science*. Vancouver, BC: Pacific Educational Press.

Rojas, C. C., and J. M. Esquivel. 1998. "Los Sistemas de Medición del Logro Académico en Latinoamérica." Education Paper 25, World Bank, Washington, DC.

Rubner, J. 2006. "How Can a Country Manage the Impact of 'Poor' Cross-National Research Results? A Case Study from Germany." In *Cross-National Studies of the Quality of Education: Planning Their Design and Managing Their Impact*, ed. K. N. Ross and I. J. Genevois, 255–64. Paris: International Institute for Educational Planning.

Rust, V. L. 1999. "Education Policy Studies and Comparative Education." In *Learning from Comparing: New Directions in Comparative Education Research—Policy, Professionals, and Development*, vol. 2, ed. R. Alexander, P. Broadfoot, and D. Phillips, 13–39. Oxford, U.K.: Symposium Books.

SACMEQ (Southern and Eastern Africa Consortium for Monitoring Educational Quality). 2007. SACMEQ Web site. http://www.sacmeq.org/.

Scheerens, J. 1998. "The School Effectiveness Knowledge Base as a Guide to School Improvement." In *International Handbook of Educational Change*, ed. A. Hargreaves, A. Lieberman, M. Fullan, and D. Hopkins, 1096–115. Boston: Kluwer Academic.

Schiefelbein, E., and P. Schiefelbein. 2000. "Three Decentralization Strategies in Two Decades: Chile 1982–2000." *Journal of Educational Administration* 38 (5): 412–25.

Schubert, J. 2005. "The Reality of Quality Improvement: Moving toward Clarity." In *The Challenge of Learning: Improving the Quality of Basic Education in Sub-Saharan Africa*, ed. A. M. Verspoor, 53–68. Paris: Association for the Development of Education in Africa.

Shiel, G., R. Perkins, S. Close, and E. Oldham. 2007. *PISA Mathematics: A Teacher's Guide*. Dublin: Department of Education and Science.

Singh, A., V. K. Jain, S. K. S. Guatam, and S. Jumjar. n.d. *Learning Achievement of Students at the End of Class V*. New Delhi: National Council for Educational Research and Training.

Snyder, C. W., B. Prince, G. Lohanson, C. Odaet, L. Jaji, and M. Beatty. 1997. *Exam Fervor and Fever: Case Studies of the Influence of Primary Leaving Examinations on Uganda Classrooms, Teachers, and Pupils*. Washington, DC: Academy for Educational Development.

Sri Lanka National Education Research and Evaluation Centre. 2004. *Achievement after Four Years of Schooling*. Colombo: National Education Research and Evaluation Centre.

Stack, M. 2006. "Testing, Testing, Read All about It: Canadian Press Coverage of the PISA Results." *Canadian Journal of Education* 29 (1): 49–69.

Stoneberg, B. 2007. "Using NAEP to Confirm State Test Results in the No Child Left Behind Act." *Practical Assessment Research and Evaluation* 12 (5): 1–10.

Surgenor, P., G. Shiel, S. Close, and D. Millar. 2006. *Counting on Success: Mathematics Achievement in Irish Primary Schools*. Dublin: Department of Education and Science.

Teddlie, C., and D. Reynolds. 2000. "School Effectiveness Research and the Social and Behavioural Sciences." In *The International Handbook of School Effectiveness Research*, ed. C. Teddlie and D. Reynolds, 301–21. London: Falmer.

Uganda National Examinations Board. n.d. National Assessment of Progress in Education. Poster, Uganda National Examinations Board, Kampala.

UNESCO (United Nations Educational, Scientific, and Cultural Organization). 1990. *World Declaration on Education for All: Meeting Basic Learning Needs*. Adopted by the World Congress on Education for All. New York: UNESCO.

———. 2000. *The Dakar Framework for Action: Education for All—Meeting Our Collective Commitments.* Paris: UNESCO.

UNICEF (United Nations Children's Fund). 2000. "Defining Quality of Education." Paper presented at a meeting of the International Working Group on Education, Florence, Italy, June.

U.S. National Center for Education Statistics. 2005. *National Assessment of Educational Progress (NAEP), Selected Years, 1971–2004: Long-Term Trend Reading Assessments.* Washington, DC: U.S. National Center for Education Statistics.

———. 2006a. "The NAEP Mathematics Achievement Levels by Grade." U.S. National Center for Education Statistics, Washington, DC. http://nces.ed.gov/nationsreportcard/mathematics/achieveall.asp.

———. 2006b. *National Indian Education Study, Part 1: The Performance of American Indian and Alaska Native Fourth- and Eighth-Grade Students on NAEP 2005 Reading and Mathematics Assessment—Statistical Analysis Report.* Washington, DC: U.S. National Center for Education Statistics. http://www.xmission.com/~amauta/pdf/ienationarep.pdf.

———. 2007. *The Nation's Report Card: Reading—2007 State Snapshot Report.* Washington, DC: U.S. National Center for Education Statistics. http://nces.ed.gov/nationsreportcard/pubs/stt2007/200774978.asp.

———. 2008. "The Nation's Report Card." U.S. National Center for Education Statistics, Washington, DC. http://nces.ed.gov/nationsreportcard/sitemap.asp.

Vanneman, A. 1996. "Geography: What Do Students Know and What Can They Do?" *NAEPfacts* 2 (2). http://nces.ed.gov/pubs97/web/97579.asp.

Vegas, E., and J. Petrow. 2008. *Raising Student Learning in Latin America: The Challenge for the 21st Century.* Washington, DC: World Bank.

Wang, M. C., G. D. Haertel, and H. J. Walberg. 1993. "Toward a Knowledge Base for School Learning." *Review of Educational Research* 63 (3): 249–94.

Watson, K. 1999. "Comparative Educational Research: The Need for Reconceptualisation and Fresh Insights." *Compare* 29 (3): 233–48.

Weiss, C. H. 1979. "The Many Meanings of Research Utilization." *Public Administration Review* 39 (5): 426–31.

Wenglinsky, H. 2002. "How Schools Matter: The Link between Teacher Classroom Practices and Student Academic Performance." *Education Policy Analysis Archives* 10 (12). http://epaa.asu.edu/epaa/v10n12/.

Willms, D. 2006. "Learning Divides: Ten Policy Questions about the Performance and Equity of Schools and Schooling Systems." UIS Working Paper 5, UNESCO Institute for Statistics, Montreal.

Wolff, L. 1998. *Educational Assessments in Latin America: Current Progress and Future Challenges*. Washington, DC: Partnership for Educational Revitalization in the Americas.

World Bank. 2004. *Vietnam Reading and Mathematics Assessment Study*. 3 vols. Washington, DC: World Bank.

Zhang, Y. 2006. "Urban-Rural Literacy Gaps in Sub-Saharan Africa: The Roles of Socioeconomic Status and School Quality." *Comparative Education Review* 50 (4): 581–602.

INDEX

Boxes, figures, and tables are indicated by b, f, and t following the page number.

accountability, 5–16
   cognitive outcomes and, 7–8
   league tables, publication of, 10–12
   of individuals and institutions, 12–14, 13b, 77
   sanctions attached to performance and, 9–10, 10b, 18, 83, 136, 141
administrative procedures for national assessment, 32–33
Africa
   capacity-building in, 87–88
   change in achievement over time in, 44, 143
   lack of resources in, 81–82, 90
   See also Southern and Eastern Africa Consortium for Monitoring Educational Quality (SACMEQ); *specific countries*
American Association for the Advancement of Science, 94
Argentina, 77, 85t, 105, 107, 128
Australia, 53, 90

Bhutan, 93, 101
Bolivia, 85t
Brazil, 17, 92, 105, 106b
British Columbia, Canada, 110, 110t
Burkina Faso, 85t

case studies, 143–44
Canada, 110, 110t
capacity building and training for planners, 87–88

census-based assessment, 3, 17–18, 25–26, 91, 126–28, 141
children outside education system, assessment of, 145–46
Chile
   accountability in, 4
   census-based assessment in, 17, 91
   corruption in, 12
   effectiveness of national assessment in policy making in, 88
   non-cognitive student characteristics in, 140
   publication of national assessment results in, 128
   resources for schools in, 91
   teacher training in, 105, 107
   Web site reports in, 63
classroom teaching, 108–21
   communication of research findings and, 109–12, 109b, 110t, 111b
   interpretation of findings and their relevance, 112–13
   learning conditions in classrooms, 141
   strategies to address problems identified in, 113–21, 114b, 122
   See also teacher effectiveness research
closed vs open education system, 5
Colombia, 67, 89
communication of research findings, 47–67, 138
   assessment data, availability of, 26, 64–66
   briefing ministers and senior policy personnel, 49–50

for classroom use, 109–12
inadequacy of, 67
individual briefings, 63
media, role of, 56–58, 129–30, 132, 134, 138
other dissemination instruments, 66, 134
press conferences, 62–63
press releases, 58–62, 60–61*b*, 133
product specification sheet, 48–49
public awareness, 125–34, 138
strategy to maximize, 130–32, 130*b*
summary reports, 50–53
technical reports, 53–56, 54–55*t*
thematic reports, 56
Web sites, 63–64, 65*b*, 128
CONFEMEN. *See* Programme d'Analyse des Systèmes Educatifs de la CONFEMEN
Cuba, 85*t*, 105
curriculum
 aims of, 1
 appropriateness of, 93
 attained, 92, 93
 belief systems underlying, 119
 contents, 94, 122
 deficiencies in teachers' knowledge of, 99
 documents, 16, 92, 111
 domains (within subject), 16, 30, 43, 92, 98–99, 110, 115
 implemented, 92, 93
 intended, 92, 93
 international assessments and, 19, 92
 materials, 80
 national assessment framework and, 98
 national curriculum (England), 9
 national curriculum (Uruguay), 93
 proficiency achievement levels and, 33, 94
 revision/reform of, 15, 56, 66, 75, 79, 92–94
 student achievements and, 16, 92
 subject areas, 8, 10, 38*f*, 50, 83
 suitability of for students, 13*b*, 16
 textbooks and, 94–95
 See also tests, curriculum domains in
curriculum authority, 50, 54*t*, 70–71, 88, 95, 138
curriculum developers, 2, 13, 35, 47, 66, 69, 70
curriculum development center, 144

Dakar Framework for Action, 7, 15
Delaware, 89–90, 89*t*
dissemination of findings. *See* communication of research findings
Dominican Republic, 84, 86*b*, 90, 105, 144

Ecuador, 105
Education for All (EFA), 37
Educational Research Centre, 50, 52*b*, 67
Egypt, 77
England, 9, 17, 128
"enlightenment" in policy-making process, 73–74, 127–28
Ethiopia, 39–40, 40*f*, 93, 133*b*
experimental and quasi-experimental studies, 78, 144–45

Fast Track Initiative, 37
Finland, 20*b*
framework for national assessment, 29, 32, 93, 98
 teacher training and, 98–99
frequency of assessment, 83, 84

Germany, 129
Guatemala, 105
Guinea, 92

high-stakes testing, 9–12, 10*b*, 14, 83, 125
Honduras, 21, 21*b*, 105
Hungary, 20*b*

identification of schools for intervention, 90–91, 139, 141–42
Illinois, 50, 51*b*
India, 81, 101, 145, 146
in-service training for teachers, 74, 97–99, 101, 104, 106–07, 107*b*.
 See also teachers' professional development
international assessment of student achievement, 3, 17, 18–20, 20*b*, 26, 32, 36, 39, 39*t*, 46, 52–53, 58, 82*t*, 90, 92, 94, 126, 129, 140–41, 144
International Association for the Evaluation of Educational Achievement (IEA), 20, 20*b*
intraclass correlation (*rho*), 35, 37
 See also student achievement, between-school differences in
Ireland
 change in achievement over time in, 43–44, 44*f*, 45*f*
 communication of national assessment findings in, 67
 recommendations following national assessment in, 114*b*
 summary reports in, 50, 51–52, 52*b*
 Web site reports in, 63, 64*b*
Item Response Theory, 17, 55*t*

Kenya, 81, 81*t*, 85*t*, 90, 145
Kuwait, 37–39, 38*f*, 85*t*, 90

Laboratorio Latinoamericano de Evaluación de la Calidad de la Educación (LLECE), 58
Latin America and Caribbean
  media reports in, 58
  public awareness of national assessment in, 128
  quality of national assessment in, 16
  teacher training in, 105
  textbook revision in, 94
  See also specific countries
league tables, 10–12
learning conditions in classrooms, 141
Lesotho, 101
longitudinal data collection design, 142–43

Malawi, 44, 82, 82t, 85t
Maryland, 83, 89
mathematics, teaching of, 87, 99, 100t, 105, 107b, 114b, 115, 129, 144
mathematics achievement, 8, 11, 16, 20b, 30t, 33, 34t, 37, 38f, 39, 39t, 40, 44, 44f, 45f, 51, 52b, 53, 60b, 63, 64b, 83, 89, 92, 95, 98–99, 103–04, 105f, 118
mathematics curriculum, 19, 52, 93, 101
mathematics test, 16, 83, 110, 111b, 146
mathematics textbooks, 94
Mauritius, 33, 34t, 85t
media, 5, 9, 47–49, 56–58, 62–63, 67, 126–27, 127b, 129–30, 131–34, 138
Mexico, 126
Millennium Development Goals (MDGs), 44
ministries of education (MOEs)
  communication of results, 22t, 46, 49–50, 58, 67
  involvement of, 22t, 95, 137–38
  policies and actions following an assessment, 69–78, 79–96
  use of assessment results, 22t, 70, 74, 113, 122, 137–146
Mozambique, 103–04, 104t

Namibia, 85t
National Assessment of Educational Progress (NAEP, U.S.)
  frequency of administering, 83
  high-stakes testing and, 9
  mathematics achievement levels, 33, 34t
  media coverage of, 132–33
  monitoring of No Child Left Behind effectiveness, 83
  press release, 59, 60–61b
  public dissemination of results, 128
  questionnaire responses, 99
  racial and ethnic data, 56, 57f
  reading achievement levels, 43, 43f
  state achievement proficiency levels, 89–90, 89t
  summary report, 50, 51, 51b
  Web site, 63, 64, 65b, 128
National Center for Education Statistics, 50
National Education Goals Panel (U.S.), 143
Nepal, 39, 39t, 85t
New Zealand, 111
Nicaragua, 145
Niger, 85t
Nigeria, 82
No Child Left Behind, 10, 83, 89

objectives for national assessment, 1, 31–32, 137
open vs. closed education system, 5

Pakistan, 101–2, 102b
Panama, 92
parents, 2, 4, 11, 13, 13b, 25, 42, 91, 93, 99, 114b, 117b, 120–28, 123f, 127b, 143, 144
PASEC. *See* Programme d'Analyse des Systèmes Educatifs de la CONFEMEN
Peru, 58, 89, 126
PISA. *See* Programme for International Student Assessment
planning an intervention, 121
policy and decision making, 69–78, 84–88, 138–39
  complexity of, 76–77
  discussion of findings, 72–73
  "enlightenment" of policy-making process, 73–74, 127–28
  identification of post-assessment policy or action, 71–75
  identification of schools for intervention, 141–42
  institutional capacity to absorb and use information, 70
  reference to other research findings, 74–75
  response to specific problems, 74
  systemwide or targeted intervention, 75
  trustworthiness and relevance of assessment information, 71, 112–13
policy makers
  involvement of, 95, 137–38
  use of results and, 2, 49–50, 74, 79, 138
political context of national assessment, 3–5, 24, 77
population for assessment, 37–42
  See also census-based assessment; sample-based assessment

preservice training for teachers, 66, 97–98, 101, 106b, 124
  See also teachers' professional development
press conferences, 62–63
press releases, 58–62, 60–61b, 133
product specification sheet, 48–49
Programme d'Analyse des Systèmes Educatifs de la CONFEMEN (PASEC), 56, 143
Programme for International Student Assessment (PISA), 36, 52, 52b, 56, 129
Progress in International Reading Literacy Study (PIRLS), 32, 35, 35f, 36
public, 25, 47, 58, 61b, 62b, 63, 69, 74, 125–34, 138
public opinion, 21, 21b, 73

Qatar, 56
quality assurance, 5
quality of assessment instruments, 15–17, 24–25
quasi-experimental studies, 78, 144–45
questionnaire responses, 99–101, 108

reading
  "engagement in," 56, 140
  national initiative, 92
  remedial programs, 75
  teaching of, 87, 94, 105
  test of, 15, 83, 146
reading achievement, 8, 11, 17, 20, 20b, 31, 31t, 32, 35–40, 42f, 43, 43f, 50, 51b, 53–54, 54t, 57f, 60b, 62b, 64, 87b, 89–90, 93, 99, 101, 102f, 106b, 115, 123f, 125, 133, 143
Reading Literacy in the United States: Technical Report of the U.S. Component of the IEA Reading Literary Study, 53
recommendations following national assessment, 113–15, 114b
reference to other research findings, 74–75
regional studies, 39–40, 40f
relevance of assessment information, 71, 112–13
reporting of national assessment, 29–67
  See also communication of research findings
resources, 5, 90–91, 95–96, 122
  description of, 80–81
  lack of, 81–82
review of education system, 84, 85t, 86b, 96
Romania, 88–89, 126

SACMEQ. *See* Southern and Eastern Africa Consortium for Monitoring Educational Quality
sample-based assessment, 16–18, 25, 26, 31t, 37, 54t, 56, 57f, 90–91, 97, 109, 113, 122, 125–28, 130
sanctions, 9–10, 10b, 83, 136
school effectiveness research, 115, 116b, 118, 122
science, teaching of, 86b, 90, 114, 115
science achievement, 8, 16, 20b, 30t, 39–40, 56, 64, 83, 92, 127, 129
science curricula, 19
science textbooks, 94
Scotland, 101
secondary analyses, 64–66, 142
seminars and workshops post-national assessment, 73
  See also in-service training for teachers
socioeconomic factors,
  achievement and, 11, 14, 128, 130
  reporting of assessment results and, 12, 14, 41, 91, 130
South Africa, 39, 39t
South Asia, 88
Southern and Eastern Africa Consortium for Monitoring Educational Quality (SACMEQ), 56, 87
Sri Lanka, 37, 38f, 85t
student achievement,
  between-school differences in, 11, 35–37, 80–81, 144
  change over time in, 1, 9, 11–12, 17, 20, 29, 42–45, 43f, 44f, 45f, 54, 55t, 83, 84, 87b, 143
  education policies and resources and, 4, 12, 13b, 31t, 32, 55, 55t, 90
  ethnic group and, 37, 56, 57f
  expectations for, 12, 16, 42, 92, 116, 117b, 118–19, 135
  gender differences in, 30, 30t, 37, 38f, 50, 55t, 64, 69, 72, 123f, 130, 135
  home/family background and, 11–14, 20, 32, 40–42, 42f, 45, 54–55, 55t, 64b, 74, 77, 112, 114b, 115, 117b, 118, 120–22, 123f, 135, 142–43
  monitoring of, 31t, 82–84, 88, 113
  proficiency levels of, 24, 30, 33–37, 34t, 36t, 50–51, 53–54, 55t, 60b, 71, 89–90, 89t, 94–95, 103, 104t, 130
  racial group and, 39, 39t, 56, 57t
  region and, 37, 39, 39t, 40, 40t, 50, 54–55, 55t, 67, 71, 80, 81, 125, 130
  socioeconomic factors and, 11, 14, 128, 130

standards of, 9, 34t, 63, 88–90, 95
student characteristics and, 12, 14, 32, 54–55, 55t, 117, 140
Sub-Saharan Africa, 23
summary reports, 50–53
systemwide intervention, 75, 141–42

Tanzania. *See* Zanzibar
targeted intervention, 75, 90–91, 139, 141–42
teacher effectiveness research, 115, 116–17b, 118–19, 122
See also classroom teaching
teachers, 9–16, 18, 22t, 24, 26, 31t, 49, 51–52, 54t, 61–63, 66–67, 70, 73–75, 77, 79, 82–83, 86b, 97–124, 127, 127b, 129, 132, 134, 136, 138–39, 142–44
teachers' professional development, 14, 18, 97, 98–108, 122, 124, 136, 143
activities to enhance, 105–08, 106b, 107b, 122, 124
national assessment framework and, 98–99
questionnaire responses and, 99–101, 108
student performance and, 99, 105f
teachers' performance on achievement test and, 101–05, 102b, 102f
See also in-service training for teachers; preservice training for teachers
teachers' unions, 4, 49, 52, 77, 126, 127b
technical reports, publication of, 53–56, 54–55t
tests
characteristics that enhance validity, 15–17, 24, 71
constructed response, 54t
curriculum domains in, 16, 43–45, 72, 80, 92, 95, 110, 110t, 119, 140
diagnostic information provided by, 56, 66, 69, 71, 72, 92, 95, 98, 110–11, 110t, 111b, 138
multiple-choice, 8, 10, 54t
rotated booklet design, 140
standardized, 113, 142
textbooks, 2, 2b, 31t, 52b, 63, 66, 74, 79, 81, 90, 91, 93, 94–95, 99, 115, 117b, 145
Thailand, 92
thematic reports, 56
time interval between assessments, 84
Trends in International Mathematics and Science Study (TIMSS), 39, 53, 99–101, 100t, 129
turnover of officials and technical experts, 70

Uganda, 85t, 109, 109b, 115, 121–22, 123f
underuse of national assessment findings, 20–24, 22t
United States
accountability systems in, 3, 5
follow-up case studies in, 143
monitoring student progress in grades 3 through 8, 83
myths about education in, 87b
public dissemination of national assessment results in, 128, 129
sanctions based on student performance, 9, 10
See also National Assessment of Educational Progress (NAEP, U.S.); No Child Left Behind
Uruguay
accountability in, 4
audience for student achievement data in, 5
availability of national assessment instrument in, 113
conflict over use of national assessment findings in, 77, 126
curriculum revision in, 93
monitoring achievement in, 83
national assessment used to review education system in, 85t
public dissemination of national assessment findings in, 126, 127b
teacher training reform in, 105–07, 107b
textbook revision in, 94

Venezuela, 105
Vietnam
outside school factors and achievement in, 40–41, 120
reading levels in, 35, 36t
review of education system in, 85t
teacher scores on achievement tests in, 101–2, 102f, 104, 105f
textbook revision in, 94
Virginia, 89

Web sites, 63–64, 65b, 128, 134
workshops and seminars post-national assessment, 73
World Bank, 88, 89
World Conference on Education for All, 7

Zanzibar, 81, 85t
Zimbabwe, 82, 85t, 90

ECO-AUDIT
Environmental Benefits Statement

The World Bank is committed to preserving endangered forests and natural resources. The Office of the Publisher has chosen to print **Using the Results of a National Assessment of Educational Achievement** on recycled paper with 30 percent postconsumer fiber in accordance with the recommended standards for paper usage set by the Green Press Initiative, a nonprofit program supporting publishers in using fiber that is not sourced from endangered forests. For more information, visit www.greenpressinitiative.org.

Saved:
- 10 trees
- 7 million Btu of total energy
- 778 lb. of net greenhouse gases
- 3,518 gal. of waste water
- 410 lb. of solid waste

www.ingramcontent.com/pod-product-compliance
Lightning Source LLC
Chambersburg PA
CBHW081231170426
43198CB00017B/2726